ABOUT THE AUTHOR

Frank Millar is London Editor of *The Irish Times*, and his journalism helped make the paper the "house-journal" of the Northern Ireland talks process. An acknowledged expert on unionist politics, he was named Irish Print Journalist of the Year in 1998 for his coverage of the Good Friday accord. His citation, penned by his friend the late Mary Holland, praised his ability and determination to understand and reflect the position of all the parties to the Northern Ireland conflict.

DAVID TRIMBLE

The Price of Peace

Frank Millar

The Liffey Press

Published by
The Liffey Press
Ashbrook House
10 Main Street, Raheny,
Dublin 5, Ireland
www.theliffeypress.com

© 2004 Frank Millar

A catalogue record of this book is
available from the British Library.

ISBN 1-904148-60-3 (Paperback)
1-904148-64-6 (Hardback)

Printed in Spain by GraphyCems.

Contents

Preface

This book was conceived in June 2004 — six long years after the Belfast Agreement, and just seven months after David Trimble's Ulster Unionists had lost their position as the majority unionist party in Northern Ireland.

I had never intended to write a book about the Nobel Peace prize winner. Indeed, I had resisted the kindly encouragement of family, friends and many contacts over the years to write any kind of book at all. However, my procrastination proved beneficial in at least one respect, for by the time I finally got my act together much of the heavy lifting had been done.

Henry McDonald's well-received *Trimble* was followed in the early summer of 2004 by Dean Godson's epic *Himself Alone*, a meticulously researched work which mines the interminable negotiations which preceded the Agreement and doggedly followed it.

Dean generously suggested that I should have written that book and I was persuaded that there remained room for a third book of a very different kind. Despite covering the process extensively I felt there were still questions about David Trimble, his motivations and the decisions he took to which I did not have adequate answers. Having watched him stretch his party to breaking point, I was intrigued by the apparent conviction of so many nationalists and republicans that the Agreement had somehow faltered because Trimble failed to "sell" it. And I was interested in the man himself, and his human as well as his political response to the strong and conflicting passions he provokes. Having left the field clear for others, might he now tell his own tale?

The morning after I asked him, a letter arrived out of the blue which clinched it. Obviously computer-generated although personally addressed, it was from The Liffey Press asking if I had a book to write or even the germ of an idea. "DT" wasn't sure he believed in omens. However, I resolved to trust this one and after two telephone conversations with David Givens I not only agreed to go ahead but, rather rashly, to hand over a manuscript on 1 September.

It obviously would never have been possible without David Trimble's extraordinary co-operation. We proceeded by way of a series of interviews in July and August fitted around the Trimble family holidays. In the final week to deadline he maintained constant e-mail contact while attending the Republican Party Convention in New York.

As Paula Goodchild transcribed the original tapes and I wrote them up, DT was able to check his answers for the purpose of correction and clarification. The line of questioning and the commentary were mine and it is a measure of the man that even where, as I am sure must be the case, he found these uncomfortable he made no attempt to renege on our deal.

First and foremost, then, my warmest thanks to him, and to his wife Daphne for tolerating my intrusions on their time and space since he became MP for Upper Bann in 1990. Likewise to David Givens and my editor Brian Langan at The Liffey Press who have been true to their word and made this such a painless enterprise.

Too numerous to mention here, and knowing many of them anyway would prefer to remain anonymous, thanks are also due to all the sources in these islands and abroad who have helped inform my work — and to my friends and colleagues in London, Belfast and Dublin who have also made it so much fun along the way.

It is appropriate to make particular mention of the Editor of *The Irish Times* Geraldine Kennedy and her predecessor Conor Brady. I will always be grateful to Conor for giving me a job I love doing. He is also deserving of wider recognition for prioritising Northern Ireland, especially in the barren times when there was little in the way of any political process there. I was equally delighted when Geraldine became Editor and immediately made clear there would be no lessening of the paper's commitment to dedicated and serious coverage of the North. I was particularly encouraged by her enthusiastic view that I should write this book. And again, her strong support has made so much of the work a pleasure.

The same must also be said for my friends and colleagues on the news and foreign desks and elsewhere in *The Irish Times*, particularly my line editors John Maher and Peter Murtagh. I am always grateful to the guys in systems for enduring my technological crises. Special mention is also due to Willie Clingan who, as then News Editor, was there into the late night and early morning hours seeing home the copy in the heady days leading to Good Friday 1998.

I am indebted to the five people who read the manuscript and provided such support. My daughter Sarah Millar road-tested the book for the hoped-for student audience and encouraged me by doing so in just two sittings. David Jordan — the former editor of the BBC's *On The Record* programme and one of the finest minds in British current affairs journalism — made particularly helpful suggestions about structure. Professor Paul Bew — a towering figure who never ceases to surprise with fresh insights and new angles — was as ever generous with his time. And I benefited hugely from Peter Smith's acute political judgement. Razor-sharp and challenging, he greatly helped me clarify my own thinking.

Immense gratitude is owed to Jonathan Caine, Special Adviser to Secretaries of State for Northern Ireland 1991–95, and one of the outstanding products of the Conservative Research Department in London. A master of the detail, with a feel for the history and theologies of the Northern Ireland Question, he generously also read the final proof and spotted most of the potential howlers. Any that remain, as they say, are my own.

For Liz, Sarah, Sophie and Catherine

Prologue

Goodbye to the Bloody Days

From *The Irish Times*, Saturday, 11 April 1998

Raw emotion, joy, wonder and disbelief swirled around Castle Buildings yesterday. And when the light of dawn came it chased away the political darkness of Northern Ireland to reveal a promise that things could be different. Frank Millar was there.

*T*HIS WAS NOT THE END, *or even the beginning of the end, more the end of the beginning. But it was still one hell of a beginning.*

They really did make history here yesterday. In joy and wonderment, and something approaching disbelief, friends and allies — and even some old adversaries — allowed themselves the luxurious embrace of fresh hope and the sense of new beginnings.

When Seamus Mallon — widely acclaimed a star of this process — rang friends early yesterday morning to share the news, the throats were strained, the tears never far away. Hardened hacks registered the surge of raw emotion as they shook his hand. It had been, in his own words, the greatest night of a long political career.

As daylight broke over the barren Castle Buildings complex in the Stormont grounds, the air was filled with the sense of something truly historic in the offing. "Think of all the bad days we've known here," said one local broadcaster. "Bloody Sunday, Bloody Friday, Bloody Monday. Bloody, bloody days. This really will be Good Friday."

Through the long hours of the previous night watch there had been no such certainty. The rollercoaster ride and lack of sleep had begun to take their toll. On Tuesday the Ulster Unionists had cried foul and threatened to walk off the pitch. Now the boot was on the other foot.

The unionists and loyalists were exuding quiet assurance that a deal would be done while Sinn Féin's Mitchel McLaughlin suddenly appeared not so sure.

Martin McGuinness had been positively scratchy at a press briefing, accusing the UUP of seeking to redirect the process and appealing to Mr Blair not to follow them down that path. In one of the portacabins, as the snow fell thick, some veterans of the peace process pondered the implications.

Could it really be? Had Bertie done a deal with Trimble and ditched Adams? Could he? More to the point, had Hume? Would he? Why would he?

At around 2.10 a.m. word emerged that the SDLP and the Ulster Unionists had agreed 99 per cent of the Strand One issues. The SDLP had apparently secured all their objectives as to the safeguards necessary for nationalists in the new

*Assembly. Asked if they had shared their triumph with Sinn
Féin, the spin doctors had been somewhat reticent.*

*Had the UUP and SDLP finally converged on the
Alliance formula — carving it up between themselves and
effectively excluding the Shinners? Between that and the
North–South bodies not being "free standing", there seemed no
way there would be an Agreement. And if there was, it
wouldn't work.*

*It was never going to be thus. The SDLP hadn't even had
to persuade David Trimble to buy the inclusive, proportionality principle. He claimed it as his own innovative approach to
a new model for government. Having clung to the local government model, the UUP had actually accepted that the Assembly should have legislative and executive powers, and an
executive committee to handle crucial business on a consensus
basis. If the Shinners were to be excluded it could only be because they elected to exclude themselves.*

*As the light chased away our darkness, there was Mitchel
signalling they had no intention of doing anything of the kind.
The miracle had been wrought. There would be a deal, and it
would carry all sides with it. This really was history. Good
history. Sweet, magical, almost unbelievable really. And then
the great rollercoaster raised itself and took off again.*

*All morning the assembled press corps had waited pa-
tiently, grateful for snippets of information about the timetable, moaning but gently about the endless delays. No matter
that the vending machine had run dry. The sun was shining,*

the snow gone, and it felt good just to be here. When it came, it would be worth waiting for.

But as the one o'clock deadline became three, then four, and the rollercoaster rose and crashed, word filtered through that David Trimble was having problems with his party. Two MPs and some officers had apparently told him they could not accept a deal putting Sinn Féin in a government "without the IRA having decommissioned a single bullet".

The "D" word was back. But it couldn't be. Could it? Most emphatically came the signal from the young briefers presumably tasked to tell us that the document Mr Blair and Mr Ahern were waiting to present to the world wasn't the one they'd agreed. Yes they had done a deal with the SDLP. But Sinn Féin's participation was meant to be conditional on the actual decommissioning of IRA weapons. Had they defined that in the Agreement? No, it was a verbal understanding, came the reply.

They could hardly be serious. Did they appreciate the pariah status that would be theirs if they did this to Tony Blair? But Mr Trimble was indeed facing serious problems. Jeffrey Donaldson was allegedly in revolt. Mr Taylor, too, was reportedly doubtful. A grim-faced Roy Beggs MP came to read the document and apparently judged it untouchable. Could they really have it in mind to overturn the leader? Would he be forced to resign before the day was out?

Irish officials suddenly found themselves in need of exercise, bumping into the journalists they had so carefully avoided through the week, presumably gathering as much information as they dispensed.

No, the UUP claims were not true. The document had not been changed. No, the Strand One deal with the SDLP had not stipulated decommissioning as a condition of Sinn Féin's involvement in the Assembly executive. No, the two leaders would not be hanging around while the UUP had a trauma. And yes, the deal would be done "because it has to be".

That presumably was President Clinton's message as he responded to the crisis, using his influence to help effect the vital last words which would enable Mr Trimble — for the moment at least — to face down his doubters.

Mr Blair gave Mr Trimble the assurance he sought that if the existing provisions to deal with office holders who did not remain committed to exclusively peaceful means proved ineffective he would support changes to make them so. And he confirmed he shared the UUP view that decommissioning measures should come into effect immediately.

The importance of words was never more plainly revealed. And on reflection, the last gasp fright may have served a vital purpose in impressing on the paramilitaries that the procession into the world of democratic government really is incompatible with the world of private armies and the dispensation of summary justice.

At the time though it seemed to add a sour note, to take some of the gloss off the occasion. And in highlighting the issue at the last lap, the UUP seemed to have notched-up still further Mr Trimble's task in selling the deal to the wider unionist electorate.

They had made history. But it was probably too much to have expected them to do it with great grace. And, again on reflection, it was maybe as well they didn't.

For in a moment of great personal triumph, Mr John Hume reminded everyone of the barriers and obstacles ahead. This was not the end, or even the beginning of the end, more the end of the beginning. But for all that, one hell of a beginning — and greater in scope, ambition and opportunity than most would ever dared have imagine.

Chapter One

The Angry Face of Unionism?

WHAT MANNER OF MAN IS DAVID TRIMBLE? Well, pretty ill-mannered actually, if you listen to some highly personal critics. "Just because he's won a Nobel Peace Prize doesn't mean he's a nice person," insists one nationalist commentator who remains doggedly unimpressed by Trimble's leadership of unionism to the Belfast Agreement and through the most troubled and turbulent days of the Northern Ireland peace process.

In his recent biography of Trimble, *Himself Alone*, Dean Godson quotes a frustrated Gerry Adams: "The thing about David Trimble is that he treats everybody like shite." And in a review of the same book Irish Senator Maurice Hayes refers to "a gracelessness, leading to a rudeness which is even more embarrassing to witness than to experience". Ouch.

The Sinn Féin president has said subsequently that he does not recognise in his isolated comment the sense of the relationship he came to develop with Trimble as some degree of mutual trust and understanding began to

8

build. However Adams would be the first to acknowledge that any regard he came to feel for Trimble was not readily understood by his own republican constituents, who regarded the Ulster Unionist leader (in their politer moments at least) as "a messer" and "a waster".

This widespread republican and nationalist complaint reflects the persistent charge that Trimble never fully signed up to the 1998 Good Friday Agreement, and that he used the recurring challenges to his leadership of the Ulster Unionist Party as a pretext to frustrate rather than facilitate its agenda for political change.

That charge has been a recurring source of frustration to Trimble loyalists, as they watched their man take endless — and in the autumn of 2003 possibly fatal — risks with his party through what they feared was in fact excessive fidelity to the Agreement. There is anger and irritation, too, at levels of personal antipathy to Trimble (among politicians, officials, diplomats and commentators) rarely displayed toward those who led the republican community through thirty years of the IRA's long "war". And then there is the simple contrasting experience of a man who — while admittedly capable of being angular and difficult — his friends also know for his warmth, generosity of spirit and general good company.

So, having endured everybody else's take on him, how does David Trimble define himself?

It is an opening question this really rather shy man finds difficult and requiring a prompt, which, as already

illustrated in the introduction above, is fairly easy to
provide.

When he was first elected Ulster Unionist leader
Trimble appeared to present the angry face of unionism
and has been described many times since as an angry
man. Is he an angry man? And what kind of things
make him so?

"I'm not comfortable with the use of the word 'angry'. I would prefer to talk about getting irritated or
frustrated," he replies. "I can remember chatting back in
1999 to Robert Bradford's widow Nora. She was remi-
niscing about the old Ulster Vanguard days in the 1970s
and saying that she thought then there was a lot of anger
in me. It's difficult for me to quarrel with that because it
is true that I have regularly got irritated. But I don't see
myself as being angry, it's a question of what irritates
me. Dishonesty irritates me. I recall an occasion when I
was speaking to a Northern Ireland Office Minister in a
corridor in the House of Commons on a very important
issue for the future social fabric of Northern Ireland. He
oozes insincerity out of every pore, never gives a
straight answer, is always twisting and turning. . . . I just
felt myself getting more and more annoyed with this
man. We might have disagreed on a matter of principle
but at least we could have had a sensible conversation.
But he was arguing constantly on a dishonest basis.
Now it's okay, I didn't throw anything at him, didn't
shout at him. But I probably started to look quite angry.

And at the end I told him I had probably made a mistake in discussing the matter with him."

This brings us to Trimble's colour. "That's another thing which I think leads people to assume that I'm angrier than I am. Apparently I colour quite quickly. I can't tell when I've coloured, when the blood has rushed to my head but apparently it does and people see me getting red-faced and they assume that I'm about to explode. Actually, I don't. In my view the occasions over my time in Parliament where I have actually lost my temper are very few."

So the history of his leadership might have been written differently, or at least perceived differently, if only he hadn't had ginger hair?

Trimble's laughter fills the room (and, yes, he does laugh a lot, and he does colour instantly). "Now look, it was really ginger when I was younger and yes I did have a bit of a . . ." He trails off as I anticipate an acknowledgement of temper. But no need to worry, our man's not making early retreat to denial. "I do remember when I was about aged five having an argument with another person and he got me so angry that I put my head down and ran at him. The other lad of course did the smart thing and stepped to one side and I ran straight into the wall."

There is more laughter when I suggest some will think he's been doing much the same sort of thing throughout his political life.

Not so much angry as irritated then, at least according to his preference. What else gets to him? "Oh, I also get frustrated with myself. There are lots of times I get frustrated with myself when I know I'm not doing things as well as I could. And sometimes, you know, even doing simple things like writing a letter can flow easily and other times it can be difficult. Or I'm engaged in an argument and I make a point and I know 'now that wasn't a good one, you've slipped up on that'."

Is his fuse very short? "Well yes and no, because now you get the other thing people also say about me. I am very cool in a crisis. It's actually when there isn't a crisis, when the boredom levels are higher, when I'm sort of half bored with things and all the rest of it. That's when things will irritate me. I'll be snappy over small things and really not when it gets to anything serious."

Yet on the "serious" things, quite a few British and Irish diplomats and nationalist politicians — not to mention some unionists — have told me they invariably found the Ulster Unionist leader a difficult man to deal with?

Trimble isn't having any of that. "I don't know what their problem is to be quite honest. I've heard some people say I'm very rude. But I'm direct, you know, I don't like beating around the bush. I remember one senior Irish diplomat — when I was making a point to him about something which wasn't exactly rocket science — and rather than engage with the argument he just

pretended and said, 'Oh, I've never heard anybody say
that.' It was so transparently false that it really did make
me very irritated. In fact on that occasion I had to put
the conversation on hold and go and get some air. But
the point is this, I'm not there to be easy for other people. And if some people find me difficult or say they
find me difficult that gives me some reassurance."

What did he make of that Gerry Adams comment?
"Well, first of all I have a slightly perverse sense of humour. I thought it was funny. And I also take the back-
handed compliment, you know. There are some people
who think that I'm just putty in Tony Blair's hands. But if
Adams is commiserating with Blair saying 'sure Trimble
treats everybody like shite', what does that tell you about
my relationship with the British government? That's at
one level. At another level I don't attach too much to it. I
do occasionally say things spontaneously but I don't
think Gerry ever does. Everything with Gerry in my
view is for a purpose. He's a consummate actor. So that
was said for a purpose, and then presumably leaked by
him for a purpose as well. But whatever about that, as
I've said to you it's not my job to be accommodating to
people, I do have to represent a viewpoint and that does
involve occasionally telling people some home truths."

Trimble sees that in different political cultures differences can be dressed in diplomatic language but says
that does not avail in this context. "The problem with
that is that you can never be sure the other fellow

decodes it properly, and especially so when you're dealing with people in the Irish system who have no real
understanding of unionist politics or unionist sensibilities. You actually have to hit them hard over the head
before they wake up and notice there's anything there. I
remember my Private Secretary Maura Quinn saying to
me early on that the problem with the Irish is that they
saw the promises from republicans at two hundred per
cent and the difficulties of unionists at only fifty per
cent. In fact I think it is generous to concede them a fifty
per cent perception."

That said, Trimble is irritated by this perception of
his rudeness: "I think I am actually quite well-
mannered. I don't deliberately go out of my way to be
offensive to people and I think I've got a bit of a sense of
humour. I also think that most of the meetings I conduct
are conducted in a good and civilised spirit and that
these accusations are made in a snide attempt to get others to discount my comments on account of alleged tem-
peramental defects."

And does he sometimes find some of these people
less than civil in their approach to him? "Oh of course,
of course. Political discourse in Northern Ireland takes
place in a different place to what it does in Dublin. I
mean, the people who complain about directness and
our being difficult to deal with should go and reread the
opening chapter of Conor Cruise O'Brien's *States of Ireland* and his comparison to the 'Kingdom of Sleek Cats'

and the 'Republic of Snarling Dogs'. These are the terms
O'Brien used to describe politics in Dublin as opposed to
politics in Northern Ireland. And there's a certain
amount of truth in that. It's part of the culture in Northern Ireland, and this isn't actually a sectarian thing, you
find it on both sides of the house, this tendency to slag
people off, the tendency to begrudgery."

So "DT" doesn't snarl any more than the other dogs
in the pack? "No. Look, it goes back to what is my position in terms of all this. I've got a particular viewpoint to
express, and in my experience those of us coming from a
unionist viewpoint have had a raw deal and an unfair
deal from the way in which other parties have behaved.
The position in the political spectrum that these other
parties were prepared to assign to us, for unionism, was
very much below the salt and indeed was scarcely at the
table. For the people who have treated us unfairly to be a
bit sniffy, and complain that we unionists are being a little angular about things, I think really is a bit rich. Now I
think you'll find it depends who you talk to. Talk to
some people in Dublin — the Department of Foreign Affairs people, some journalists — and they'll say I'm difficult. But if you are talking to people I actually deal with,
if you talk to Paddy Teahon, for example, or the Taoiseach Bertie Ahern, they wouldn't say that. And if you
talk to people in London you'll get a bit of a mixture too.
There were people in the Conservative government I had
uneven relations with. And, yes, okay, I've had uneven

relations with some people in the Labour government. But I think you'll find if you speak to the bulk of people in the media and in government in London you'll get a different reflection. What people get from me will also to a large extent be a reflection of what I get from them."

What about David Trimble's wife and children, I wonder? Might they recognise him as a difficult man? The colour rises again with the laughter: "Well, aye, they've seen me being difficult at times. I don't know that they've been on the receiving end but I'm sure they will have seen me get irritated at times."

But it hasn't been wife Daphne's unannounced mission to refine her man or soften his hard edges? The thought clearly strikes him as hilarious. "Well if she has, she's done it in such a diplomatic manner that I have not been conscious of it. But that's not to say it hasn't happened, you know," he replies, still laughing.

ABOVE ALL, THAT IMAGE of the unsmiling Trimble harks back to the mid-1990s and his role as champion of the Orange Order's "right to march" down the Catholic Garvaghy Road in Portadown. The political compromises he has made in the intervening years have actually made it perilous at times for Trimble to walk freely the streets of Portadown and other areas besides in his Upper Bann constituency. Is he still an Orangeman or is that association now a political embarrassment?

He confirms that he remains a member and still walks with "the Brethren", though not on anything like the scale he once did. "I was actually more than a little annoyed with BBC Northern Ireland on the Twelfth of July two years ago," he recalls. "I was walking with my private lodge in Bangor, County Down, and the Beeb had a camera crew there when it came my turn to take 'a lift' of the banner. So there was I — I think I was First Minister at the time — carrying the banner and the BBC crew got excited and came charging along the road to get a good vantage point and film me doing it. I said to the fellow who was carrying the other pole, 'You're going to be on the [TV] highlights tonight.' But they never used it. I was more than miffed at that."

Trimble's catholic taste in music has been well-documented over the years. However, people might be surprised to find it extends to marching bands and the annual "provocative swagger" which so many in Britain and around the world think so damaging to the interest and reputation of unionism. Registering my surprise at his apparent continuing enthusiasm for all that, Trimble concedes: "There are aspects of the way in which the Grand Lodge is conducting itself that I think not in the best interests of Orangemen. But I'm not going for that reason to leave people who've been my friends for over thirty years and something which is and will continue to be a very significant aspect of social life."

They may understand the social aspect of the Order. But people reading this — who've lived through the political traumas of the past ten years, and whose first

introduction to Trimble might well have been via those
scenes at Garvaghy Road — may find it difficult to
square the political stance he's taken with his continued
membership of what they would consider an anti-
Catholic organisation.

Unsurprisingly, perhaps, the politician and lawyer
has a take on Orangeism which might not be recognised
by many Catholics or, for that matter, by plenty of Orangemen either. "The Orange Order came into existence
over two hundred years ago. It was a religious order
within a very political context and it expressed something that was very close to the identity of the Ulster unionist in those days. In a sense in the course of the last
decade or two Roman Catholicism has changed enormously and the theological grounds on which Orangemen and politicians would have disagreed with the
Catholic Church are in a different context."

In any event Trimble asserts: "There is nothing in
any way in terms of the nature of Orangeism which
makes co-existence with Catholics and nationalists impossible. Indeed there are things within even those basic
statements of Orangeism that were written in the 1790s
which do prefigure the basis of co-existence."

But did he not run the very real risk just a few years
back of finding himself expelled for attending a funeral
mass? The lawyer has studied the rule book, which in
turn occasions a first reference to his political hero.

"This is a matter which I think a lot of Orangemen misunderstand. There was no problem with regard to Sir James Craig attending funeral masses, which he did on a number of occasions. There is no law in the Orange institution which says you must not do so, now that's not generally known either. There is the well-known passage in the 'Qualifications of an Orangemen' and in my private lodge, in addition to the normal ritual, we always got somebody to read out 'the qualifications' at each meeting. For some reason every time I attended that's what I got asked to do, and I don't think that was for any reason other than that it is fairly lengthy. Anyway the qualifications is not a set of laws, it's . . ."

It's the one requiring members not to countenance any act or ceremony of "Popish worship" isn't it?

"Yes," he confirms. "There is such a reference in the 'Qualifications' but it's aspirational, it's aspirational that the qualifications talk about personal conduct and demeanour, attending to church worship, not swearing, not taking up other aspects of personal life and so on, but none of those are laws, none of these are things that would lead to expulsion. So there are I think some Orangemen of a somewhat bigoted disposition — which I don't attribute to their membership of the Order but to other things — who misinterpret this."

Trimble then tells an amusing story centred on Banbridge, in his constituency. Towards the end of the Second World War a large number of Belgians were stationed there training for the Belgian army. As a result of the close relationship arising from this, every year a number of Banbridge councillors go off to attend some ceremonies in Belgium, during which they have found themselves attending a Catholic Church service. This has been going on since 1950 and the bulk of local councillors during this time would also naturally have been Orangemen. "Year after year they went with no questions asked — until one of the local Lodges fell out with one of the councillors for some unrelated reason. They were looking around, and they were going to try and get him for the fact that he went to this Catholic service as part of his civic duties. So he reminded them of all these precedents and nothing came of that. But eventually they got him for attending a fundraising event for a local school one Sunday because there is actually a provision in the Laws of the Orange Institution on Sunday sport. Then, as if to seal his fate our friend compounded the offence by handing out the prizes at this event, explaining that he had only done so because by that stage of the afternoon the priest was too drunk to do it himself."

Membership of the Orange Order would, of course, have been pretty much obligatory for anyone previously aspiring to lead the Ulster Unionist Party. That said, many an ambitious fellow down through the years might have done little more than observe the ritual, even perhaps while privately telling his more "respectable" friends he found it all a bit of an anachronism. Trimble plainly does not belong in that category. But I want to pursue the question of his beliefs further, for it has been suggested that this provincial politician turned metropolitan sophisticate no longer attends church. Is that so?

Trimble has read the same suggestion and is clearly exercised by it. "Yes I do, I regularly attend church. I am not personally very active in the church that I attend, although nearly all the rest of the family are. And National Presbyterian in Washington regards me as their furthest-travelling member."

Tony Blair once famously cringed when Jeremy Paxman asked if he and President George W. Bush prayed together. Trimble is more than happy to worship in Washington. And when in London he and his family go to Crown Court Church of Scotland. He quickly adds that this is popular with the family for the added reason of its proximity to the well-known and highly rated Orso restaurant in London's Covent Garden. Unburdened by "Protestant guilt" or fundamentalist strictures, the Trimble family will happily follow the communion service with an excellent lunch and a bottle of red.

Indeed he recalls one occasion when the service had been particularly long and he led the family through London's streets "at a rate of knots" to be sure of saving his table at the even better-known J. Sheekey's restaurant. Charging through a small alleyway he sighted one of the Rev Ian Paisley's senior colleagues who had obviously spent the morning, not in church, but enjoying Covent

Garden's excellent shopping facilities. After the chance encounter Trimble would regret not having taken the opportunity to stop and introduce his family on their way from Church: "This amused me enormously but unfortunately I was just in too big a hurry and too focused on getting to lunch to take advantage of the situation."

Such little episodes can assume huge significance in unionism's vicious internecine warfare. But this one also leads us back to the big questions. Is David Trimble a religious man? And what part does his religious belief play in his politics? Are they part and parcel of the same thing or can he separate them?

"I try to separate them," he replies. "And I don't like people in politics who make great play of bringing religion into it. I think that it is a fatal mistake for unionism to reduce the issue in Northern Ireland to sectarian terms. Repeatedly, and it's consistently shown over time — you see it thrown up in the 'Life and Times' survey, and it doesn't move much — a significant percentage of Roman Catholics in Northern Ireland, round about eight per cent, identify themselves as British. Given the choice of describing themselves as Northern Irish or Irish they say they are British, culturally British. Actually I think the percentage is higher but for political reasons they'll be reluctant to put it in those terms. There's then a further ten to fifteen per cent of Northern Catholics who regularly indicate that, in the event of a referendum, they would vote for remaining in the United Kingdom.

"To some extent this might be considered a somewhat crude judgement about relative economic advantage. But it's more than that actually, it's about the wider
horizons they have as a result of being within the British
State and consequently being able to move with easy acceptance into other parts of the British State. In fact
Northern Catholics who are domiciled in England and
Wales have a higher social profile than southern Catholics domiciled in those countries. That's a rather interesting thing you get from analysis of the census figures. So
you've got this percentage who are culturally British,
and/or tactically British, and to drive them away from us
is just utter folly. Indeed one of the great criticisms historically of the Ulster Unionist Party from the 1920s onwards is that it did tend to drive them away. It was more
open to Catholic involvement in unionist politics and
they were more flexible in that respect pre-1920. And
then unionism also missed a huge opportunity in that
respect in the 1960s. So I think it is a mistake for us to allow politics to be reduced to sectarian headcounts, although it is true that religion is probably the single best
guide to voting habits compared to any other factor in
Northern Ireland."

Trimble thus acknowledges that there is a sectarian
basis — which he does not intend in the pejorative sense
— to social life in Northern Ireland and that "this is
likely to continue in the indefinite future". But while this
"significant social force" should not be ignored, he says

"we make a mistake to turn that into a key defining issue of politics".

Most people will find little remarkable in Trimble's political calculations, although it strikes me that he rather readily accepts the reality of the North's sectarian base and does not appear to define its destruction as a priority of his political project.

But getting back to the question of personal belief, Trimble implicitly explains his reluctance: "I dislike people who in the course of the way they express themselves in politics keep bringing in religious terms. This gets back to the old saying that 'the more he talks of his honour the faster we count the spoons'. It may very well be that some of those who, when they're on a political platform, start bringing religion into it are personally sincere. But I always feel it rings false and I hardly ever do that, I don't feel comfortable doing that."

Then he reveals himself: "At the same time I have to say I don't think I would have done all the things I have done in the last half dozen years if I wasn't absolutely sure in my own mind that it was the right thing to do."

It simply isn't David Trimble's style to claim to have been doing "God's will". But this is a compelling confirmation that, in some of the quiet watches of the night, the Ulster Unionist leader counted on a power greater than himself. It is also a powerful retort to those political rivals and enemies who routinely invoke "the Lord" on behalf of their cause, the more so for the quiet and plainly reluctant manner in which it is confided.

Seizing my own Paxman moment, I ask him: Do you pray? "Yes, from time to time. I can't say that I do so often. But in 1998 [the year of the Agreement] and the following year I had a very strong sense that this is what I should be doing." Where his laughter had previously filled the room, the silence was broken now only when a visibly moved David Trimble cleared his throat before retelling an event that reinforced that sense of what he should be doing on the eve of the crucial meeting of the Ulster Unionist Council in November 1999 at which he asked his party for the first time to enter into government with Sinn Féin.

"I arrived home on the Friday evening before the meeting. I had collected the mail from the letter box that morning but as I was going inside I looked at the box and there was a letter there, unstamped and obviously hand-delivered. I opened it up and found it was from Nora Bradford encouraging me to go for it." The following morning before the meeting started, Trimble showed the letter to the late Josias "Joe" Cunningham, then President of the ruling Ulster Unionist Council. "He looked at it and said, 'That's very good.' But Joe was a man of taste and he then said, 'But you wouldn't use that, would you?' So I assured him, 'No, no.' Subconsciously, however, I must have been hoping to use it because during the meeting a number of references were made to people who'd been murdered by republicans. Specific references were obviously made to Edgar Graham and Robert Bradford, and during my summing-up of the debate I also mentioned their names when, lo and behold, somebody just handed the opportunity to me on a plate. I heard this big 'gulder' from the body of the hall and immediately recognised it was John Hunter [a one-time Trimble loyalist who broke with him over the Agreement]. I stopped and let him be heard until he accused me of betraying Robert Bradford . . . then I pulled Nora's letter out and I read it. I don't know that it really changed anybody's mind. But the reason I'm mentioning it in this context is that when I went back home I realised this was bound to get out, or at any rate get back to Nora. So I picked up the phone and told her what had happened. She in turn told me that she'd been sitting at home on Friday afternoon and had a strong sense that God was telling her to write a letter to me." Mrs Bradford wrote that letter and travelled from her home in Newtownabbey, across Belfast to the Trimble residence outside Lisburn, hand-delivered the letter and then returned home in a journey that would take her several hours. "Aaaah. . . . It's the sort of thing that reinforced my sense of 'this is what I should be doing'," concludes Trimble, his eyes again seeming moist, his voice strained.

Alastair Campbell once famously said of his Downing Street press operation on behalf of Tony Blair: "We don't do God." Well, David Trimble has just "done God" (or at

least come as close as he's ever likely to) with a modesty
and intensity which is as impressive as it is surprising.

I have watched and reported this man as closely as
any journalist through the years of his leadership. I have
criticised his decisions and questioned his judgement,
often sharply. I have enjoyed access at key moments in
crucial negotiations such as at Hillsborough in the
spring of 1999 while Tony Blair, Bertie Ahern and President Bill Clinton pressed him to critical decisions and
potentially crippling compromises, and I have admired
his coolness under fire. And I can quite literally feel the
importance of this moment in this conversation, for he
has shared something which his every instinct will tell
him he does not wish to see reduced to print.

The savagery of the internal unionist debate in
Northern Ireland can exact a heavy price from those
who allow uncertainty or doubt, or attempt to see the
other side's point of view. Like his many predecessors,
Trimble has had to battle against — and seemingly in
the end fallen to — a rival unionist leader, the charis-
matic Rev Ian Paisley, whose fundamentalist beliefs (at
least in theory) brook no room for compromise. Yet here
is a powerful testament which any man of the cloth
would surely have to acknowledge, at least for its au-
thenticity. The agnostics among us may look away,
thinking that the Almighty has featured much too
prominently in the politics of Northern Ireland. But
Nora Bradford is a woman of faith. She lost her hus-

band, himself an evangelical clergyman and Member of Parliament, to IRA assassins. Yet she believed God wanted her to write to Trimble at that crucial moment urging him to make peace with the representatives of those who had left her widowed. And one doesn't have to agree with him, or with the political judgements he made in that time, to understand better from this the weight those tough calls forced on David Trimble and the courage they required of him.

Chapter Two

The Unionist Moderniser

THE CONFIRMATION OF DAVID TRIMBLE'S strong religious belief and adherence still to the Orange Order brings us back to one curiosity about his leadership which has been previously identified.

Admirers observing his political struggle from afar may have had the notion of Trimble, the previously angry man of unionism, having experienced a Damascene conversion on the way to Stormont on that Good Friday morning in 1998. And in their not particularly well-informed but well-disposed way, they will have approved what they would regard as Trimble's conversion from unionist hardman to champion of peace and reconciliation between the two communities in Northern Ireland. Yet the point has been made that — while free of any sectarianism in his personal and professional dealings — David Trimble has always been and basically remains a tribal leader.

He resists this on several counts along the way, explaining that, while there were not many Catholics

where he grew up in Bangor, County Down, his
mother's decisions on the suitability of playmates for the
boy David would more likely have been based on considerations of class rather than religion. Although both
liberal and generous, Mrs Trimble "would have regarded herself as very middle class". He recalls cutting
his first political teeth canvassing in the now republican
redoubt of Andersonstown for the moderate unionist
politician Basil McIvor in then Northern Ireland Prime
Minister Terence O'Neill's famous "Crossroads" election
in 1969. And while more attracted to Stormont ministers
of the period like Brian Faulkner and Bill Craig (whom
he would later join in Ulster Vanguard), Trimble explains that their appeal for him was that they were actually the "modernisers" of their time when compared to
the "rather effete" and aristocratically connected
O'Neill. Faulkner, too, moved from perceived hard-liner
to power-sharer. Craig of course became a nationalist
hate figure as he challenged Paisley for the hard-line unionist vote, inspecting the massed ranks at Vanguard
rallies, threatening and portending a violent loyalist response to the IRA terror which followed the Civil Rights
campaign with its original demands for justice and
equality and an end to anti-Catholic discrimination. But
again, Trimble reminds us that Craig eventually made
his own dramatic bid for a political accommodation with
nationalists in 1975, when he proposed a "voluntary coalition" government for Stormont. And while observing

that the IRA's direct assault on the state of Northern Ireland made it difficult, and at times impossible, to sustain — David Trimble has no difficulty divining a connection to his own modernising tendency, even through the difficult years which saw him champion the Orangemen's cause in Portadown and join a rooftop protest at a visit to Belfast by the then Taoiseach Charles Haughey.

Yet even after he confounded his nationalist detractors and delivered the Ulster Unionist Party's support for the Belfast Agreement, the charge persisted that he never graduated from being the leader of unionists, never quite transformed himself into "a First Minister for all the people of Northern Ireland". This is despite the fact that in 1998 he recast Sir James Craig's famous depiction of Stormont as "a Protestant Parliament for a Protestant people" in pledging his commitment to provide "a pluralist parliament for a pluralist people". Indeed, the implication sometimes has been that he was never really in the business of reconciling the two sides at all. In *Himself Alone*, Trimble is quoted as telling the SDLP's Sean Farren that what he really wanted was to do a deal with the other side which would then enable his own people to be left alone.

Trimble recalls that encounter differently: "I recollect the question was 'What do your people want?' And I said they want to be left alone. And peace in that sense, giving them peace, you know, is about not interfering with them, not pushing them around and making them do things they don't want to do. One wanted peace, in the first instance, in the sense of an absence of politically inspired violence."

But are people wrong to think he had no great interest in building bridges across Ulster's sectarian divide? "Yes," he replies, before offering his own explanations as to why they might nonetheless have that impression. "There is a reason why people have the other perception. I'm keenly interested in history and obviously have an interest, for example, in some aspects of the history of the Orange Order . . . and there's no point trying to deny the fact that what you have in Northern Ireland is a division which goes beyond the division between Conservative and Labour. Now it's a division that carries with it somewhat different social systems, built on different churches, with in many cases also different national identity perceptions and even different national allegiances. That is so and I respect the other allegiance, I always have respected the other. It's not mine, it's not where I am. I must say I've never thought of Irish nationalism as being attractive. I have my own views about the behaviour of Irish nationalists, even some views about Irish nationalism as a concept which aren't entirely complimentary to them, but there's no point in me going on about that. The point is there are people who do not share the same sense of identity and history and who move in social organisations which are different from mine, and I think what you've got to have first and foremost is an element of mutual respect and toleration."

Warming to his theme, Trimble continues: "I'm not going to go in for some false bonhomie, I always think when other people go in for this sort of bonhomie that there's an air of falsity about it and I feel uncomfortable about it. I do want to see the absence of conflict, which is the first step, being replaced by a situation where people are comfortable with themselves and with each other. But I'm not going to pretend that they've ceased to be what they are, or that they are now something else, or that we can easily throw away the old labels and old identities and adopt something else. There have been times when I have flirted with ideas like that, but I ended up concluding that that was not feasible. So getting to a situation where people are comfortable with the society they live in, even though they choose to construct their own personal social life in a particular pattern, is, I think, the best you can reasonably expect in this situation."

But this doesn't mean he was content just to be a tribal leader and had no interest in reconciling the two communities? "No, but the people who've got a concept of reconciliation which is that we've all got to pretend to be best friends, you know, and live in each other's pockets all the time. . . . I'm pretty sure they don't do that in their own lives. I don't think what they preach for others is what they practise themselves. Nor is it reasonable to expect other people to behave in that way, as if it comes down to a sort of political correctness that we use a certain language even though it's not what we actually do and we know it's not what people believe . . . where if we can sort of compel everybody to use this particular language then everything's okay, isn't it? And it's not."

Trimble explains: "I have my own views as to what was likely to happen in the longer term in that situation [following the Agreement] and I did not see it as being a situation which led to an accentuation of national feeling as such. In fact, I thought we were more likely to ameliorate those matters and more likely to gradually evolve to a society where people were more comfortable and where the differentials would be less of an issue. Differences in society, differences in religious belief and identity are not necessarily a bad thing. In Great Britain we have lots of different religions, lots of different community identities, even national identities. And that's not a problem because, touch wood, they are not aligned with current political issues, whereas in Northern Ireland there is a very strong alignment between current politics, the clash of political views, and religious and national identity. Now community relations problems come as a result of that. To go and deal with those problems alone, and to focus on community relations problems alone, is to look at symptoms rather than causes. What you should do is try and defuse the political clash and have a situation where we no longer have religion and community identity coaligned with political views.

If you defuse that political clash then the problems that come from different religious belief and identity are quite different and then become quite soluble. That is why I think the cure for this problem is long term."

Trimble also saw the evolution to a more civil society being assisted by the fact that the religious elements were and are transmuting or changing. "Vatican II changed the Catholic Church enormously, moved it actually in terms of its practice and its behaviour much closer to Protestant churches. In the Protestant churches too, whereas a generation or two ago you'd have had some fairly sectarian approaches to matters, that is diminishing an awful lot. And it's the way in which, despite what might have happened in '69/'70/'71 and in fact over the years and the troubles, the churches have got closer together. . . . I think with the increasing secularisation of parts of life, and indeed with the churches adopting some of the social mores of that secularism even if not becoming secular themselves, then you're going to get a different society evolving. But the idea that you could somehow compel people to adopt a different pattern of life I think was not realistic, and to insist on a form of organised hypocrisy was actually counter-productive."

Trimble explains himself further: "The fact that I'm sceptical about how much can be done as of now to deal with problems that undoubtedly exist in community relations does not mean that I shouldn't try by some measures of a more practical nature. And here, growing out of the experience we had in North Belfast, very much the view that we needed a completely different community relations policy whereby — rather than just promote activities to bring both sides together, which usually tend to end up in middle-class areas or involving children — you actually look at those parts of your society where there is a serious problem. And that is mainly at what are known as the interface areas. Then you ask, 'What can we do to defuse the tension at the particular interfaces?', which is what we were doing when we developed the North Belfast Community Action project. What I would have liked to have done had we remained in the administration was broaden that out throughout the rest of Northern Ireland and try to get local communities and local councillors involved. Because it is local people who have to solve these issues. And I think if there is a restoration of devolved government we are going to have to come back to this interface problem. In terms of everyday living in Northern Ireland, with the reduced level of violence, reduced level of threat, society is functioning normally, except at the interfaces. So I think we've got to have a focus on that. But the focus I'd want would be very practical, very much related to what local people on the ground can do, are doing, and less of this airy fairy approach where 'nice' folk come along and talk down to people."

While some critics would no doubt be happier with a bit more "airy fairy" and to hear Trimble lapse into what he considers "political correctness", this I think provides a clearer and much more positive indication of his approach to the questions of sectarianism and the need for reconciliation between the two communities.

Might he also then clarify one other aspect of his character? The title of Godson's biography — *Himself Alone* — was I think an intended compliment to Trimble as a remarkably self-contained and self-reliant political leader. Yet it has probably also reinforced a quite different sense that Trimble is a loner. Is he? And has he found leadership a lonely experience?

He agrees that "self-contained" is right: "I've always been fairly independent. At an early age my mother complained that I'd always do things in my own way." However, he goes on: "I don't see myself as deliberately wanting to be a loner, although I have to say I'm a person more for quiet company than for the crowd. So I suppose yes, independent, self-contained. I think 'loner' is a bit of a pejorative term and I don't see it as being appropriate. I have actually enjoyed politics enormously and there's a fair amount of conviviality in politics, a fair amount of getting together and I enjoy that. I also enjoy having breaks from that, particularly when I get to London. There are evenings I would just spend quietly by myself." But he's not at all a lonely man? "No, I don't see myself in those terms. I can be sociable when I put my mind to it, but it doesn't flow that naturally and I have to acknowledge that. And I am shy and that is a problem."

Not least because of his shyness, one thing has long intrigued me about David Trimble — and that was his absolute certainty back in 1995 that if he declared for the vacant Ulster Unionist leadership he would win it.

I had been puzzled to find most commentators in Northern Ireland already writing him out of the contest to succeed James (now Lord) Molyneaux as leader following his retirement on 28 August.

Soon after his election to succeed the late Harold McCusker as Upper Bann MP in May 1990 a surprisingly large number of senior party officers had told me they already considered the parliamentary new boy "the likely next leader but one". Even if he now assumed the media and establishment favourite John Taylor (now Lord Kilclooney) would first be given his turn, therefore, it seemed to me he would surely want to enter the race if only "to put down a marker" for the next one.

As it turned out DT particularly welcomed my telephone call that August night, for he too had been surprised (and I guessed more than a little miffed) at finding his possible candidacy dismissed out of hand by journalists who apparently had not bothered to check his intentions with him.

In a joint story with my *Irish Times* colleague Dick Grogan I duly reported that Trimble might indeed be a leadership contender, and then waited while he made up his mind before calling again to check the position.

From the soundings I had taken in the interim I was fully ready for Trimble to tell me there was sufficient evidence of support to persuade him to throw his hat in the ring. However, what I was not prepared for was his absolute certainty that, if he did, the leadership would be his. "I haven't made my mind up yet," he groaned, before adding: "I don't know if I really want to be the leader." I humorously suggested that was not necessarily the decision he was required to make at this point, to which he immediately responded: "Oh no. I told Daphne last night, 'You do realise if I go for this I will win'."

Reminding him of this conversation, I ask him how on earth he knew? He acknowledges having made the prediction before offering slight resistance: "I know that comment, there was a certain overstatement in that. I didn't actually know." I can see why he might say that now but he sounded good and certain at the time. "Well, people were encouraging me to do that and I was I actually sort of saying to Daphne . . . 'You do realise if I go for this I'll win?' Yes, but I was saying, 'Let's take time to stop and think.' I didn't think it was actually for certain that I would win. I knew I would do very well. Before the meeting I did search around for what I thought would be a very useful thing to say in an acceptance speech. So I prepared that although I thought it was tempting fate to do too much work on that."

But why was he allowing himself to think like that? What told him the delegates to the Ulster Unionist

Council might prefer him to the media favourite John Taylor or the establishment candidates in the form of Willie Ross and the Rev Martin Smyth? Trimble's analysis reveals the complexity of his own position and of the choice confronting the UUC delegates at the time. "There was in fact just one of the contenders, and it's sad to say this, who was totally out of the running, and that was the Rev Martin Smyth. Five people went for it, and there were four real contenders. Willie Ross, who was Molyneaux's man. Ken Maginnis, who was the 'liberal's' man. Then you had Taylor — who's probably more a loner than I am although he can be convivial too when he wants to be — but who was always regarded as a bit of a maverick. And me, and I suppose I was regarded as a bit of a maverick as well."

Trimble laughs uproariously when I confirm he certainly "got that one right" and tells how former party secretary Jim Wilson approached him in 1989 after his unsuccessful attempt to win the party's nomination for the European Parliament. "He took me aside and asked 'Why are you always on the margins of the party?' to which I responded, 'I'm always there because people keep pushing me to the margins. I don't particularly want to be there, you know.'"

Yet there he was barely six years later pretty darned sure that if he allowed his name to go forward the same people would elect him leader? My surprise was that much of the media had written him off when he might

reasonably have been expected to put down his marker
for a subsequent contest. But whatever he might say now,
he had already moved to another place. He had been close
to certain the crown was already his, hadn't he really?

It is at this point that Trimble reveals that the question of the party leadership had in fact been in his mind
since before entering the House of Commons in the
spring of 1990. "The folk in Upper Bann who approached me to stand as candidate there told me that
they were choosing the next leader of the party and they
were going to me because they thought I was the person
to be the next leader of the party."

And within a year of finding himself an MP, Trimble
found this assessment of his future prospects had spread
from Upper Bann to Westminster. "Within a year or so
after the by-election, I had the sense that most people (in
London) regarded me as a substantial figure. Within a
year or so I think if you'd done a poll you'd have found
that people who had taken interest in Northern Ireland
in and around Westminster . . . most of them would
have told you the same thing, that they expected me to
be the next leader of the party. I was not unconscious of
that opinion. And funnily enough I thought somehow
that that would actually have its own way of seeping
back to people at home."

Trimble acknowledges he was helped on his way by
his increasing media profile. However, he also confesses:
"And I'm afraid there's an arrogant bit in this too, of

looking at those people [the parliamentary colleagues], and thinking, 'All fine fellows but I'm better than any of them.' I thought that. I'm sure it's not what I'm supposed to say. I also thought Taylor was the best of the lot and I was comfortable enough to be Taylor's number two. In fact originally I thought that was the way to put myself at the centre of things without having too stressful an existence myself because actually being number one has things on the downside."

Trimble then seems to say he was more or less committed to standing all along as he recalls the impact of a conversation with some of Molyneaux's Lagan Valley delegates on the very morning their MP confirmed he was standing down. "One woman delegate bumped into me around lunchtime really upset. 'What on earth are we going to do if you don't go for it?' she demanded. 'You have to.' I was left in no doubt that she regarded it almost as part of the contract I had made with the party to be available for it. So all of that left me feeling not only that this could happen but this is highly likely to happen. And then once we started to go for it, when we started telephone canvassing, I kept saying to people, 'Stop getting carried away, these returns are just too good.'"

For while all the indications were good, Trimble's reservation remained "that I could hit a ceiling, you know, because of this 'maverick' business and not having as long a record in the centre of the party as other people, that while I would pick up a lot of support from delegates who were not office holders I might then hit a ceiling at which point the party establishment would then unite behind one of the other candidates."

He needn't have worried. By the close of business in the Ulster Hall on the evening of 8 September David and Daphne Trimble, whatever they might have intended, were the new establishment. And for reasons and in circumstances they could scarcely have imagined that night, they would come to count on the old party establishment they had so derided to sustain them. But does that very change in circumstances — the agreement to enter government with Sinn Féin without IRA decommissioning, and the consequent alienation of the so-called "Young Turks" who had supported his leadership bid — mean that the Ulster Unionist Council delegates elected him that night on a false prospectus?

David Trimble doesn't think so, but he knows why I'm asking. The perception holds to this day that he won the leadership after his triumphant march down the Garvaghy Road with Ian Paisley and the jubilant Orangemen that very summer. He had earned his points as a hardman at the precise moment when the UUP hierarchy was concluding that Molyneaux had to go because he was too close to John Major and the then Conservative government. If Molyneaux was thought to have grown too fond of warming his toes at the Downing Street hearth, the delegates surely didn't elect Trimble to succeed on the promise that he would be even more accommodating to London. After the British and Irish governments had produced the Downing Street Declaration in December 1994, and the subsequent Framework Document in February 1995, the unionists had decided Molyneaux's long leadership had grown weak, and Trimble promised a much tougher alternative. Isn't that so? I mean, he didn't seek the leadership on the promise that he would be a softie?

"Oh no, no I'm not saying that. But what I did say was that I was going to make a serious effort to make political progress and that I was not going to follow in the pattern of sitting back and being defensive. I made it clear that I'd go anywhere and talk to people and take that quite different approach from Molyneaux. But the essential point to my mind in what I said to the party was that the 'do nothing, sit in our entrenched position approach' wasn't mine, that I was going to carry the argument to others and I was going to try and achieve progress. And progress in 1995 meant doing a deal because our declared policy from 1986 onwards, under Molyneaux, had been to seek an alternative to and a replacement of the 1985 Anglo-Irish Agreement.

I can easily understand the Upper Bann people deciding to elect Trimble as MP already thinking him a likely future leader. They had enjoyed high-grade representation by Harold McCusker and would have been more aware than others perhaps of the importance of presenting a reasonable face of unionism to Westminster and the wider world. But while the official party policy may have pre-supposed a new deal, there is surely something of Trimble's subsequent problem here. There were certainly people inside the unionist party who understood the need to "talk the talk" and to present a positive image but who never ever thought for one minute there was any danger of having to deliver. And having concluded Molyneaux had got too close to government, these people were among those electing Trimble in the belief that he would not run the same risks. Were they not bound in the end to feel the same disappointment with him as that suffered by Thatcher and the Tory right, who elected John Major to succeed having convinced themselves he was "one of us" only later to discover that he never had been?

Trimble has a very different perspective. "Well now, look at the track record that they will have looked at. Trimble who was with Craig in voluntary coalition, indeed some of them suspect wrongly that I was the author of that idea. Trimble who is regularly chatting to officials at the Northern Ireland Office. Trimble who with Craig and David McNarry produced a policy paper in the late seventies which turns out to be the blueprint for Jim Prior's 'rolling devolution' plan, which was my idea. They knew where I was with that. Trimble who — when Paisley was trying his hand at moderate politics in the Atkins' conference in 1980 — where I was actually tracking in that direction and there was a sort of a joint unionist approach. Trimble — who wasn't for going down Molyneaux's integrationist path, which he saw as being part of the 'do nothing, let's dig ourselves into our trenches' policy — but was instead going for devolution. And everybody knew, even if I hadn't fully internalised the concept when Bill Craig first mentioned voluntary coalition in 1975, that the need was to do a deal with nationalism. By 1995 the only question was the shape of the deal, if you were going to do one. And so they [the UUC delegates] would have known that the perception of me in the party was much more as a dangerous moderate than as a hard man."

Trimble understands that the moderate image was not much on display during the crisis generated by the Anglo-Irish Agreement in 1985. "I actually saw the Anglo-Irish Agreement coming, and from a different perspective from others, and that's why when the Ulster Clubs were being formed I went along. I remember going to a first meeting actually and someone advised me to be careful because a camera crew was filming people going in. I went out of my way to make sure I was seen, and said to people, 'Look, the Northern Ireland Office think I'm a moderate and if they realise that moderates like me are moving to this position it must have an impact on them.'"

So there was no basis for a misunderstanding? "I'm not saying that but I am saying that a lot of the people in the party, people like Willie Ross and Molyneaux, never trusted me. And what they distrusted of me was not extremism but the fact that I might move the other way. So there was that element there. Now the liberals who supported Ken Maginnis saw something else and thought I was way off somewhere else. I've never quite understood that but that's where they were. You have to draw a distinction between different audiences. Some of the people casting their votes at the UUC would have been influenced by Drumcree in a positive way. But some would certainly have been influenced in a negative way, not least because I had associated with the Democratic Unionist Party. And, you know, back in 1990 when I was seeking the Upper Bann nomination, the biggest problem I had was having been involved in that demonstration against Charles Haughey. That was the biggest problem I had when I was speaking to the branches and the delegates."

Trimble describes his involvement in what became known as "Drumcree One" — after the RUC Chief Constable banned the Portadown Orangemen's traditional annual post-church service parade down the nationalist Garvaghy Road — as accidental, and certainly not calculated. He says he knew his association with Paisley would be damaging in the eyes of many party colleagues. At the same time he concedes that "within the broader unionist community, yes, there were undoubtedly people who watched the events at Drumcree and thought I was going to be their man, 'doing something'." But he goes on: "They were the people who didn't see that all the time we were at Drumcree I was trying to do a deal with the police, exploring any opportunity for compromise, and at the rally that was held delivering what the *Irish News* described as a speech of 'impeccable moderation'. And on the second Drumcree, what was I doing? Going to the Cardinal and the church leaders and trying to get them to broker something."

I had always taken the view that Drumcree placed Trimble in an impossible situation, and that politically he had no choice but to back the Orangemen given that this was happening in the heart of his own constituency. That's certainly how he saw it: "I had no choice in the circumstances."

And when the delegates to the UUC came to elect a leader he is satisfied he did not offer them a false prospectus? "I don't think so."

Yet he didn't tell them explicitly what was already at the back of his mind, namely a warning by his constituency agent John Dobson that he would have to deal with Sinn Féin?

Again laughing, Trimble says, "When John said that to me some time before the leadership election I certainly did not indicate assent." Then he explains: "We're actually in the post-ceasefire situation, and I don't at that stage in September '95 have a clear picture of where the politics is going, and nobody then I think had an idea of the extent of political support for Sinn Féin and the extent to which that would increase. So yes, Sinn Féin and the republicans were moving into the process. One didn't know exactly where that was going to go but I didn't think at that point that it was going to go as far and as fast as it did. And yes, I'm thinking primarily, 'We're going to have to do a deal with Dublin and with the SDLP.'"

Trimble knew he had to deal because of his political inheritance from Molyneaux and the fact that unionism's position had grown weaker over the years. "The status quo was not an option, to borrow a phrase, was not desirable from our point of view. Just at the tail end of the talks that Molyneaux and Paisley had been involved in during 1991 and 1992 I could see the outlines of a potential agreement with which I wasn't entirely comfortable. And I do actually think what I got in '98 was better."

Long before Trimble assumed the leadership it was widely held that unionism, in only ever seeking limited reform and change, invariably offered "too little, too late" and arrived at the talks table only to discover that the nationalist agenda had moved on. Trimble also believes that Molyneaux, heavily influenced by Enoch Powell, made a fatal early miscalculation in his dealings with Margaret Thatcher when he decided to boycott the 1979/80 talks hosted by then Northern Ireland Secretary Humphrey Atkins.

"I thought this was the height of folly because his position almost implied that he wanted Thatcher to impose his preferred solution [for one or more regional councils in the North] on everybody else. That was never going to happen because the events from 1968 had shown that a

degree of nationalist consent was necessary for any institutions in Northern Ireland. The events at Sunningdale in
December 1973 [which resulted in the power-sharing
government and Council of Ireland, toppled after a brief
life by the Ulster Workers Council strike in 1994] had
shown that the Irish government could not be excluded
completely from the process, or at least that the British
would not exclude them. So therefore to think you could
get Thatcher imposing something was folly. There would
have to be engagement in a process which included the
unionist objective with, of course, no guarantee our objective would be achieved. But rather than attempt that,
Molyneaux took up this stupid business of boycott,
thinking he could force her back down his chosen path,
and of course that spectacularly backfired and she went
off in a totally different direction."

Molyneaux himself described the subsequent Anglo-
Irish Agreement as representing "the beginning of the end
of the Union", certainly as unionists had known it. Was it
really as bad as that when Trimble assumed command?

"I knew the one thing unionism could not do was to
allow itself to continue to be marginalised, it had to get
itself back onto the centre. Now, initial reaction to the
Anglo-Irish Agreement was very, very gloomy, and one
read the contents as being about creating a situation
over a decade or two where people wouldn't be able to
tell whether they're in the United Kingdom or the Republic of Ireland, the implication being that Britain

would somehow tiptoe away. So yeah, very, very gloomy. On the night of 15 November 1985 and on the morning after, it looked bloody awful. In fact, I think there were not many unionists on that day who thought the Union [with Britain] would see in the new century. But then a sense developed that after having done the deal the British government, after a year or so, was walking away from some of the assumptions in the Agreement. In other words it was settling down to be something less threatening — not because the terms had changed in any way but just in terms of actual implementation. There was on the British side a degree of caution and maybe even a degree of disenchantment. I know that Thatcher ended up disenchanted and of course there is evidence for this now from her memoir."

But the trend of Anglo-Irish diplomacy was nonetheless established. Whatever its limitations from a nationalist perspective, the 1985 Agreement had, as Trimble puts it, "put the British/Irish partnership at the centre of policy-making and further marginalised the unionists".

Then, too, through the final Molyneaux years and into Trimble's leadership the situation was further complicated when it emerged that John Hume was in dialogue with Gerry Adams and that they were developing a peace initiative.

Molyneaux was the subject of some serious ridicule when he later characterised the emerging peace process as potentially threatening to the unionist position. Could

Trimble at least understand where his predecessor was coming from in respect of Hume/Adams?

"Well, yes, because many unionists saw the business of the IRA moving away from violence toward politics as a signal that they could achieve their objectives, that they were going to achieve their objectives, by other means. Following the first IRA ceasefire in 1994, the instinctive reaction of unionists was to think, 'The IRA wouldn't have done this if there wasn't a secret deal.'"

Trimble says he was always sceptical about that possibility: "I was very much of the view at the time that the IRA were being defeated. There was always push and pull with this business of republicans coming into politics. The push was the success of the security forces and the disenchantment of the core support the IRA had relied on. There was a pull factor, too, in the attraction of politics and the possibility of political success, and that started for them at the time of the IRA hunger strikes."

So while not necessarily as fearful as many other unionists, Trimble believed Molyneaux and Paisley had wasted a decade before realising they had to engage with the British government — and even then found themselves playing catch-up because the Hume/Adams dialogue meant the caravan was again moving on rapidly?

"Look, if Paisley had done the deal that was there for him in the talks convened by Thatcher's first Northern Ireland Secretary of State Humphrey Atkins in 1980, I would have supported that. Indeed, David McNarry,

James Cooper and I publicly endorsed Paisley's participation and criticised Molyneaux for his boycott of those talks. And when everybody (Molyneaux, Powell, etc.) was congratulating themselves after Thatcher's "Out, Out, Out" rejection of the main proposals from the New Ireland Forum on 19 November 1984, I knew they were in a fool's paradise. One was frustrated at a situation where opportunities were being missed and because of that the situation was deteriorating. It didn't follow that I thought it was bound always to deteriorate or that it was a one-way course and would never change. But I felt there was a hand for us to play that wasn't being played."

So he didn't arrive at the table with what has been called a "defeatist unionist" mentality? "No. If you were defeatist, if you thought there was no hope of ever changing things, then the best you could look for was managed decline. And there was an element of that in Molyneaux's leadership. I thought actually we could change things for the better and I set out to change the perception of unionism. I wasn't ever going to settle for managed decline, and that demanded a different approach, which led to where we are. I think now — whether this is just my own mythologising — that even though I didn't spell out the detail, and even though I didn't anticipate all that would follow from it, that was the basic prospectus I was holding out to the Ulster Unionist Council in 1995. And I think that's a large part of the reason why they stuck with me."

However Trimble saw the situation, of course, many nationalists and republicans signed up for the Belfast Agreement precisely because they believed it was wholly and completely about enabling unionists to manage their own decline and ultimately accept their destiny in a united Ireland. Trimble is adamant both that he "never saw it in those terms" and that nationalists and republicans who did got it wrong: "I saw myself in negotiation clawing territory back."

Did he ever think that Tony Blair saw it in terms of managing unionism's decline? There is a long, and I suspect a somewhat revealing, sigh before Trimble answers this: "I don't know that he actually thinks these things through in those terms. I think his political horizons are fairly short term, always."

Trimble refers to the Prime Minister's family connections in Coleraine and Tyrone while he thinks further through his assessment of Blair's motivation. "He's actually familiar with the province. I don't know how far that actually informs his approach, and maybe knowing of that makes me a little bit too indulgent or too prone to put a good construction on what he's doing. But I don't get any sense that he saw or sees it in terms of managing [unionist] decline. I mean, go back to that first speech he gives in Belfast, May '97, where he talks about the consent principle, addressing some primary school children in the audience and saying he doesn't think there will be a united Ireland in the lifetime of anybody there. That was actually ad-libbed, that wasn't in the text. Now maybe he just got carried away by the occasion. . . ."

Or maybe the real high politics of that first visit to the North was that the new Prime Minister had to act quickly to assuage unionist opinion because he and Mo Mowlam were planning to bring Sinn Féin very quickly into the negotiations?

Trimble counters this, telling me to bear in mind that he and his colleague David Burnside had been passing outlines of a possible agreement through intermediaries to Blair from early 1996, long before his first general election victory. They were saying to the man who would be Prime Minister, "Here is a deal that can be done, and we are up for a deal."

But it was still at that point to be a deal between the Ulster Unionists and the constitutional nationalist party, the SDLP? "Oh yes," comes the confirmation. "Even in April '98 the deal was the SDLP, it wasn't Sinn Féin. But in terms of where we started out in this discussion, in terms of perception of what was achievable. . . . I did think, notwithstanding the Anglo-Irish Agreement, that it was possible to change our position from being marginalised to being more central as players in the political process in Northern Ireland but also nationally in the United Kingdom. I didn't think we were in managed decline. I did actually think it was possible to create a situation which would be more stable and more unionist-friendly."

Chapter Three

Guns and Government

IT WAS THIS BELIEF THAT HE could bring unionism back from the margins which carried David Trimble through the tortuous negotiation which led to the Belfast Agreement. He has frequently characterised its achievement for unionists as twofold: the acceptance by all the sides of the principle of consent, and the consequent participation by republicans in a partitionist settlement. But has he not greatly exaggerated this "achievement", and paid a heavy price for it, because "consent" was there in the Anglo-Irish Agreement in 1985 and has in fact been the operative and guiding principle of British government policy since it was defined by Edward Heath's government as far back as 1973?

Trimble's memory and knowledge is greater than mine and he takes me further back: "Oh, you can go further back than that because consent is the operative element of British government policy, as and from 1920. It's not clear until 1920 that consent is British government policy. The reason why unionists organised the way they did in 1912 to 1914 was because they feared their consent was going to be ignored. But a fair bit of the political establishment was veering towards consent by 1914 and by 1918 they were at that point and it is written into the 1921 agreement that created the Free State. So in that sense consent is there, and in that sense too the Irish Free State in 1921 and again in the 1925 Tripartite Agreement clearly bought into consent. But then de Valera repudiates consent. John Hume never actually gets his head round the concept. The Irish state in Sunningdale in 1973 does not accept consent. The Anglo-Irish Agreement gets to a sort of a fudge position where people say 'there will be no change in the status of Northern Ireland without consent', but without defining what the status was and without asking people to consent to that Agreement. It's sort of saying, 'We're going to impose this upon you but we promise we won't impose anything else'. Now there's a certain credibility lack in that and of course our shibboleth in this is Articles 2 and 3 of the Irish Constitution, which laid claim to the territory of Northern Ireland irrespective of the wishes of its inhabitants. So one of the things that is undoubtedly an achievement of '98 is we get change in Articles 2 and 3, and in fact the Agreement writes a double consent provision into the Irish constitution. There has to be a separate consent in the Irish Republic to the admission of Northern Ireland to a united Ireland, which was their idea, not ours. I find that fascinating. So you get consent then coming into the Irish constitution and you get consent being accepted now by the SDLP, I believe, in a wholehearted way. And when the SDLP subsequently start to try and develop a language of a post-nationalism I think that's genuine on their part. The fact that they [later] allowed themselves to be scared by the Shinners didn't help."

So it's consent of a very different quality, augmented or made real by the withdrawal of Ireland's constitutional claim? "It's the withdrawal of the claim, and the formalisation of consent, approved by the people north and south in the dual referendums. That I think does change the context quite significantly. But it's not just that. I think there were other things that we did. We got a new architecture and completely neutralised the whole issue of cross-border stuff, and we've got cross-border structures and arrangements now that actually work satisfactorily and don't cause any problems for us. They are largely symbolic from a nationalist point of view, that is significant.

"What I thought was the big thing and what I kept going over in all the meetings we had with the SDLP during the talks was that our two parties were the centre of gravity in Northern Ireland and what we had to do was work together. I kept pressing them on that. Subsequently I talked about our two parties providing 'the voluntary coalition' within the compulsory coalition. I thought the thing was only going to work if the SDLP and us worked closely together. Part of the reason why, on the very last night when we were signing off on the internal devolved arrangements, that I go a little further than some people thought I should in terms of conceding the title of minister and a few of the other 'safeguard' provisions to the SDLP was because in my mind the business of entering into a genuine partnership between us and the SDLP was the core of this. If I'm curmudgeonly and grind them down in negotiations, there's the danger that they become easy prey for Sinn Féin, but there's an even bigger danger that they become resentful of me and of our approach to it. This is the start of a partnership between the two of us and we've got to do it in terms of being friendly with each other. So at the point when I abandoned my preference for 'departmental secretaries' and conceded the term 'ministers', Hume actually burst into tears and they all started throwing their arms round us and that seemed to me to be laying the foundation for what was going to happen. But it doesn't work out that way as you well know."

One of the big mysteries for me through all of this has centred on this question. Why — having as he saw it done "the big thing" for the SDLP, and agreed to the full legislative Assembly and Executive demanded by them, as against the Welsh Assembly/regional administration model favoured by his own party — did Trimble not go for a weighted majority by which the Ulster Unionists, SDLP and the Alliance Party would exercise executive power? Under such an arrangement Sinn Féin would have been handed the prospect of power but would first have to work their passage and overtake the SDLP. Why instead did he not only construct a bridge to bring republicans "in from the cold" but a bridge which would bring Sinn Féin into the Stormont cabinet office in one fell swoop?

Trimble counters that it was Molyneaux who had "saddled" him with the d'Hondt formulae which would subsequently be used to allocate the ministerial jobs between the qualifying parties, and that this principle of "proportionality" had been UUP policy since 1992.

But come on. In all fairness to Jim Molyneaux, he and his colleagues certainly weren't talking about putting Sinn Féin in government back then? "No, they weren't. But they weren't talking about excluding them." That, surely, was because the suggestion of including them had never arisen in 1992. Wasn't the real point anyway surely that Trimble consciously decided to include them when he agreed the basis for devolution in 1997?

Trimble recalls hints by Molyneaux, the Rev Martin Smyth MP and others that they could envisage talking to Sinn Féin after a period of "quarantine" and is anyway insistent: "I want to put the record straight here. If you look back at the Unionist Party proposals for the Strand One talks in 1992, about the purely internal Northern Ireland arrangements as part of any settlement, it's d'Hondt."

Yes, but nobody until the final week of negotiations in April 1998 had the faintest notion that he was talking about a full-blown government that would include Sinn Féin?

Trimble is determined, as he has argued over the years, that a fully inclusive and proportional arrangement was in fact part of his bequest from the Molyneaux/ Paisley talks with earlier British governments. "No, no, no. It's perfectly obvious from '97 onwards that when they [Sinn Féin] come into the process, having won so many seats in the Forum, that if you stick to proportionality. . . . Now we have hung our hat on proportionality from '92 and for five years we'd been banging on about proportionality. If I suddenly turn round and say, 'Whoops, changed my mind, I don't want proportionality, we'll go for weighted majorities instead', and it's obvious that you're doing it to exclude Sinn Féin, it puts you in a slightly queer pitch in the matter. And our effort in the negotiations is to try and link proportionality to things like decommissioning. But let me say this: to have a link to decommissioning so that Sinn Féin doesn't get the advantage of proportionality until they have genuinely done the business."

So you were thinking they would probably still be excluded because you didn't expect them to do the business and qualify for office?

"That was one of the factors that we had in mind during the negotiations and of course when it came, and we see the final draft at the end of the day, the biggest thing was that the linkage between holding office and decommissioning wasn't as strong as it should be."

I still don't quite get this. It is possible now to forget the magnitude of the policy shift with which Trimble was proposing to bounce his party. In a final repudiation of the Molyneaux years he had agreed the creation of a powersharing government at Stormont, in which John Hume or Seamus Mallon would serve with him as co-equal First and Deputy First Ministers. Having conceded to the SDLP, surely all he had to do was take Hume or Mallon aside, explain the facts of life as he saw them, and reason that while he could win party backing to share power with the SDLP he would be wasting his time if Sinn Féin had to be part of the equation? Why did he not seek at that moment to detach the SDLP from Sinn Féin and go for a centre-driven government?

"Well, we thought we were doing that. Okay, this may be one of the things which in retrospect one would have to pin down more clearly. But this was about constructing a good relationship with the SDLP. We also left the SDLP in no doubt about our position on the linkage between IRA decommissioning and the rest of it. Now implicit in that is the position that, if they do decommission, yes . . . I went to see unionists in some parts of the west of the province who would say to me in one breath, 'Oh I can't have Sinn Féin, can't, terrible', and then take a pause before adding, 'The SDLP are no different from

Sinn Féin at all'. Wait a minute, hold on, where are you on this? And there is also the fact you have got to bear in mind that if the republicans are actually turning their back on terrorism and coming into the political process then what is the difference between them and the SDLP?"

Most unionists of course saw a world of difference between the SDLP and Sinn Féin. Trimble has said himself he saw the republican movement as being in transition but wasn't at all sure they would complete it. In an interview with *The Irish Times* in April 2000 Trimble expressly rejected my assumption that somewhere along the path of his original tactical engagement in the talks chaired by former US Senator George Mitchell he had made the leap of faith and accepted the bona fides of the republican leadership. If he wasn't convinced of their unequivocal commitment to purely peaceful methods, why on earth was he considering bringing them into government at all? Why not pursue the other option and push the SDLP to go it alone with the unionists and Alliance? At the very least why not put the SDLP to the test?

Very deliberately he tells me: "I don't think that was a viable option at midnight on Thursday 9 April 1998. The structural issues on Strand One [the internal arrangements for the governance of Northern Ireland] had all essentially been pre-determined even before the Mitchell talks began in 1996. Go back to the talks unionist leaders had with Secretaries of State Peter Brooke and then Sir Patrick Mayhew circa 1991–92 and the agree-

ment on Strand One. Now the agreement wasn't final-
ised but the broad shape of it was, and we went into the
'96 talks with our '93 position, which was based on
d'Hondt and with the principles of proportionality and
automaticity at the heart of it."

But that UUP policy was hardly drafted with power-
sharing with Sinn Féin in mind, I persist. "I know that, I
know that," Trimble replies now sternly. "But let me explain to you the situation as I saw it. We go into talks
largely bound by the power-sharing mechanism that
had been developed in '92. There isn't a formal executive in the '92 model but we knew that there was going
to have to be movement in that direction because we
knew that the model that we were sticking to in '92 was
unworkable, let alone not being acceptable to other parties. And I mean all through '92 and again through '96
and all the rest of it, people knew we couldn't even have
run Belfast City Hall by this model. In City Hall we do
have a General Purposes Committee which effectively is
the executive. So we're going to have to have something
there. Now to turn round at the last minute and say,
'Hey boys, because we've Sinn Féin in the process I'm
going to tear up everything and start from scratch',
would have destroyed the process in any event. But
there's another factor, and this is where you might have
a different view of me. It comes back to where you are
with regard to what is happening with republicans.
Where they were as I saw it in the '90s, particularly

when we had the revelation of the secret contacts with the British in 1993, was that the penny for a variety of reasons was dropping with republicans that violence was counter-productive, that quite apart from the moral considerations it just wasn't going to work and was making the situation worse. Worse for them as well as worse for others. And that the republicans were in the process of dropping the armed struggle. If republicans dropped the armed struggle and engaged purely in ordinary politics, even if they still remained totally committed to a united Ireland, that is a hugely beneficial thing, right? And that's why then when we got to '97, our position vis-à-vis republicans was predicated on the basis that they would move to being a normal political party. And if they did that, then it would not be right to exclude them from the benefits of the structures that had been already tentatively agreed. So the emphasis then was really not on excluding republicans but rather on getting republicans to complete the transition and excluding them if they didn't deal with the transition. That is quite a different position, and that basically is the position we were in."

That seems clear enough. David Trimble didn't quite believe Gerry Adams and co. when the Agreement had to be concluded — but he wanted to believe them and he believed they should enjoy the full benefits of an unequivocal embrace of politics. But wasn't the problem that would come to haunt him — and finally prove his electoral undoing — that he failed to make the linkage to IRA decommissioning, the scrapping of IRA weapons and the completion of the republican transition, a condition within the terms of the Agreement everybody else signed up to?

"That was the huge problem with the Agreement, no doubt about that. Our position through the negotiation of the Agreement was that republican participation in the Executive should be made conditional on decommissioning."

Yes, but the problem was that he didn't succeed in making it a condition of the Agreement. He may have wanted it but he went ahead with the Agreement anyway and accepted a procedure which, assuming Sinn Féin got enough votes, would entitle them to seats in government. He also accepted an "exclusion" mechanism which — because it would require "cross-community", that is to say SDLP, support for any action against Sinn Féin in the event of the IRA defaulting on decommissioning — people knew from the outset simply wasn't going to work. Isn't that the reality?

"But wait a minute. That was the huge problem on 10 April, because our position was that republican participation is conditional on decommissioning, right? And then we get a linkage which is not robust enough, where the high degree of probability is that it wouldn't have worked. I couldn't have said with certainty, but looking at it we sort of say, 'This is the weak point.'

David Trimble: The Price of Peace

Now that was the position on the afternoon of 10 April 1998, because when we worked through everything else we were left with two issues: prisoner releases and IRA decommissioning. And by decommissioning what we had in mind was the linkage of decommissioning to holding office. That was the whole point of it. And when we had to decide which was the key issue, we decided the key issue was this. Then the question for us is, 'Are we going to say, simply because of this, there will not be an agreement?' — bearing in mind I was coming from a position when I accepted the leadership of having a unionism that was marginalised, a unionism that was losing out steadily?

"When Mo Mowlam arrived in '97 she said the status quo was not an option and some people were getting excited, and I said, 'Look, the status quo's not an option for us either because the status quo post the Anglo-Irish Agreement was the status quo where unionism was weak and marginalised, where the system was being run for the benefit of nationalism and the long-term effect of that was going to be disastrous from the point of view of the union with Britain.' And if we were going to get ourselves back into the centre and have any hope of clawing back ground, we knew we were going to have to make a deal. We knew a deal was going to involve difficulties. But the question we had to look at on that Friday afternoon was whether we would be better off or worse off accepting the Agreement. And the view of most, with difficulty and with reluctance, was that we would be better with the deal. Now, there was the problem about the linkage of decommissioning to holding office. But I didn't regard, and I don't regard, the Agreement of April '98 as being Holy Writ. I knew there were unresolved issues that we were going to have to have a fight over in the period afterwards. And I was looking at the situation, thinking, 'We've got a number of things so far on this, we don't want to throw them away, and we've got outstanding problems, we want to position ourselves' . . ."

I interrupt at this point just to clarify this. Does this mean that after all the presidential phone calls from the Clinton White House, after Senator Mitchell flew home to his wife and young child, after an exhausted but delighted Bertie Ahern returned to Dublin and a jubilant Tony Blair finally got to join his family for their Easter holiday in Spain — and while news of the historic breakthrough was greeted with acclaim across the world — David Trimble did not regard himself as yet committed to sitting in government with Sinn Féin?

"No," he tells me. "Look, on that Friday afternoon there was a fair probability that Sinn Féin would reject the Agreement, and Sinn Féin did not actually accept the Agreement on 10 April 1998."

I interject again with what may appear a stupid question but which to me seems blindingly obvious. Whether Sinn Féin would finally accept or not, whatever about their procrastinations, their "need to consult the republican base" and all of that, why couldn't the condition Trimble sought be made explicit in the Agreement? Why couldn't he just say, if it was what he thought, "God almighty, these people or their pals have been murdering members of my community for thirty years; we're talking about bringing them into a government, and the Agreement must be explicit that the IRA must do X, Y and Z within a designated timeframe if Sinn Féin members are to hold office before I go anywhere near my party with this deal"? Would nobody else go along with that? Did the Ulster Unionist leader even ask them?

"At that time of the day, yeah, at the time we saw the draft with its weak linkage. Now I've mentioned what our position was in terms of there having to be linkage. When Jeffrey Donaldson and I went to Chequers a couple of weeks before to prepare for the last bit of the negotiations, there was agreement that there had to be a provision excluding Sinn Féin if they didn't decommission."

Are we talking here about what became known as Tony Blair's "side-bar" letter after the Good Friday accord was concluded? "No, no, before we got on to that. What I'm saying to you is this. When Jeffrey Donaldson and myself left Blair and John Holmes [Blair's Private Secretary at the time] at Chequers on that Sunday afternoon we understood all four to be agreed that if Sinn Féin did not decommission they would not go into the Executive. So it wasn't a matter of weighted majorities or anything like that. We were expecting a mechanism that would do that. Now I don't have this in writing but that's where we were at Chequers, that's where we were in the run-up to and through the last week of the negotiation. At times we would remind the British government that of course we have to have an exclusion mechanism — 'Yes, yes we're agreed on that' — and then when it emerges it emerges in a weak form. Five of us go up to see Blair late in the afternoon — and by the way this is long before any telephone call from Bill Clinton — and we say this is the problem, we need an effective exclusion mechanism, and Blair says, 'Look I can't unravel this now, everybody is . . . you know . . . this is where we are, we can't change this document now.'

So Blair suckered him? "I don't know if that is true or not," Trimble admits. Yet if this was such a big thing — and he and Donaldson had left Chequers understanding they were all agreed on the exclusion mechanism — how come they were only seeing it inadequately presented in the final text, on the last day, and when it was seemingly impossible to change presumably because the other parties would not agree to do so?

"Because there weren't texts until late in the day. There was the earlier Mitchell text which we said had to be binned or dealt with, and this was one of things that had to be dealt with. Did Blair sucker us? I don't know, he may very well have been genuine both at Chequers and in the last week. Whether he did or he didn't, I then made the suggestion of the side-bar letter."

The essence of this letter was a promise by the Prime Minister that if the exclusion mechanism in the Belfast Agreement proved inadequate, he would bring forward legislation to change it. Most people thought at the time, and think still, that the letter was no more than a last-minute attempt to cover Trimble's embarrassment and was otherwise of no value or significance since it was not included in the text of the Agreement itself or endorsed by the other parties as forming part of the Agreement. David Trimble holds to a very different view.

"The letter was my idea, and it was the same idea that I used to solve a problem over the Strand Two talks about the future relationship between Northern Ireland and the Republic. And it wasn't even new then. It goes right back to the original concept of 'rolling devolution', and beyond that. I reminded people of what happened in 1921–22, following the Government of Ireland Act 1920. Elections to a Northern Ireland Parliament in May of 1921, some powers devolved in December '21, other powers over the course of the six-month period after that, and security powers not actually devolved until May '22. I was saying, 'Have your election, and then use your post- election period to resolve issues.'"

So the "Agreement" concluded on the Good Friday was really just a work-in-progress? "Yeah, but what that was doing was using the period post the election to solve the problem. Now before I put that idea to the Irish on the Wednesday night, I spoke to British officials, and I asked what they thought was a likely period of time between the Agreement, the referendums, the Assembly election and the earliest point at which power could be devolved. And they said they couldn't see power being actually transferred before February '99. So I was working with that, saying that there was going to be this period from May through to the subsequent February — nine to ten months, something like that — in which these issues could be sorted out. Now that was Wednesday night. Then we come to the Friday afternoon, we're at a situation where we've got a lot of good things in the Agreement, the Agreement is on balance in my view a good thing for unionism, and we've got this problem over decommissioning. If they do decommission, then yes, it's fine for them to be in the Executive, but we've got to get the decommissioning. I said I was looking at the period post the election to solve this issue. And that's why, when Blair said he couldn't get the thing renegotiated, I asked for commitments from him to be in a letter which I thought would strengthen our hand post the Agreement in order to achieve this."

But what status or authority did Trimble think that letter carried? "Well, you see, that's why I was so anxious to have the letter circulated, that's why when Clinton phoned me I said, 'There is this idea which might solve our problems but I need the nationalists and the

Irish to back off', because if they had dumped on it and said, 'We don't agree with that, it means nothing', then we wouldn't have had an Agreement. The letter was important, but it was important not just as a means of easing the party into taking a decision, but important for what was to be done in the post-election period."

Important to him and the Ulster Unionists clearly. But, again, what was its status? According to Trimble: "Its status was an authoritative interpretation of the Agreement, of the decommissioning section. Someone actually did say to me afterwards that we should have gone to court over the whole decommissioning question at the time when republicans and others were saying, 'Oh, there's only an obligation to use their best efforts, they don't actually have to do it.' Which if they'd thought about it is a contradiction anyway. Some people did say at the time to go to court to get an authoritative judicial interpretation of the decommissioning section of the Agreement because that did impose an obligation on republicans to decommission."

What, the Blair letter? "No, the Agreement itself did. I think the proper interpretation of that clause requiring the parties 'to use any influence they may have' to secure the disarmament of all paramilitaries was just a good faith clause. The section as a whole says that they commit themselves to achieve total disarmament and that put an obligation [on them] and the Blair letter confirms that interpretation."

The British government did indeed subsequently confirm this view in terms. Mo Mowlam said that while IRA decommissioning was not a precondition for Sinn Féin entering the devolved government, decommissioning was "an obligation" under the Agreement.

If the Ulster Unionists and the British government were broadly of the same view, and republicans disputed it, why didn't he then go to the courts?

"If you're going to any sort of court, whether a British court or an international court, to say what is the impact of the decommissioning section of the Agreement, then the court would have determined there is an obligation to achieve decommissioning, total disarmament, permanent, of all paramilitary organisations, by such and such a date. So that bit of the letter about the interpretation I think was legally significant. It has to be said too that the British government, and I think arguably the Irish government, never resiled from the position that decommissioning was an obligation. That's actually important, particularly for those unionists who, driven by their own ambition, were going around saying, 'There is no obligation to decommission.' I really was infuriated at the time with the hypocrisy or stupidity of the people who were saying this."

But it wasn't specified in the Agreement as a prior requirement for Sinn Féin joining the Executive. And I put it to Trimble that he was forced in the end by that simple fact, and by the logic of the argument, to "jump first" and form the Executive in November 1999 without any decommissioning taking place.

"Oh, I don't think I was forced by any logic, the logic of any argument, to do that. I don't think that was at all in my mind. In my mind Blair delivered on the letter, and he did so twice. The first way he delivered on the letter was in the Northern Ireland Act 2000, by introducing legislation giving the British government the power to suspend the Assembly. The whole issue comes back in the spring and summer of 1999, when we've reached the end of the transitional period so far as making arrangements for creating a new administration and still no decommissioning. We get republicans to accept in the spring of '99 that they have an obligation, we don't actually get them to do anything. And then Blair's saying, 'The only way we're going to achieve this is by setting up the institutions.' He's come back to the 'linkage'. We say, 'Well, we're quite happy to set up the institutions if the Shinners are not there.' At the time when Blair came to meet my Assembly group, they were pressing him on this, and Blair's response always was, 'I can't force people to serve on the Executive.' Now, decoded, that means, 'If I legislate to exclude Sinn Féin, SDLP will refuse to serve.' He wasn't saying 'I can't exclude', he was saying 'I can't force people to serve'. That is the origin of the legislation to suspend. He said, 'The best I can do is to have a mechanism that rolls everything right back to the status quo ante if they don't decommission.' He was saying to us at that time, 'We believe there's been a seismic shift they are about to decommission but they'll only do it immediately after you've formed the Executive.' We were saying we weren't going to go in beforehand without there being a certainty of them decommissioning. The certainty that Blair could offer us was, 'Well, if they don't decommission, we'll go back to the status quo ante.'"

But however he rationalised it, the massive downside for David Trimble was that he would then be damned for abandoning the "no guns, no government" policy on which his party had fought the Assembly election. No matter in the first instance that it was for just six weeks before he forced the first suspension of the Assembly. Having vowed that he would not, Trimble "jumped first" and was seen to go back on his word and, crucially, to have lost the argument. Wasn't this the moment that marked the beginning of the erosion of trust which would finally see the rival Democratic Unionist Party triumph in the second Assembly election in November 2003?

Trimble delivers a cold and steely dismissal of this analysis. "But I never went back on my word. I never abandoned my 'no guns, no government' policy. Maybe I should have but I never did, and when there were no guns I made sure there was no government. And when DUP people say to me now, 'no guns, no government', my reaction is, 'What the hell do you think the position is? We've actually got some guns and there's no government because they didn't give enough guns and they didn't do it in the right way.' So as far as that phrase is concerned, I regard myself as having stood absolutely on the principle and maintained that principle at some cost to myself right through the negotiations preceding the election in autumn 2003 until now. Funnily enough, the people in the DUP who accuse me have in their policy papers floated as an option going into a form of government in the Assembly with no guns at all, and without there ever needing to be any guns given up."

As Trimble sees it, he joined battle on this issue that Good Friday afternoon even before the ink was dry on the Agreement. "I knew there were battles still to come, that there was going to be a battle over putting the IRA out of business. But for me on 10 April 1998 having an agreement — yes, with that battle still to fight — was much better than having no agreement, and the world blaming me for there not being one."

I'm pressing hard on this because many people have never been able to comprehend the UUP failure to tie decommissioning to Sinn Féin's entry into government explicitly in the body of the Agreement. Likewise, they could not believe that the highly controversial provision for paramilitary prisoner releases was not similarly tied to disarmament. Why wasn't it?

"Hold on a second," comes the sharp reply. "I didn't . . . the Agreement did." Really? How so? "Oh, the

Agreement isn't a legal document, again that's another mistake a lot of people make. They assume that this is a big legal document and they're looking for the certainty that a conveyancing lawyer would have about anything."

Is it not an international treaty signed by and binding of two sovereign governments? "And how many treaties are precise, without their opacities and all the rest of it? This is actually very clear. Look, a two-year period for decommissioning, a two-year period for prisoner releases. It's obvious, you really have to be stubborn not to see ..."

But surely the two-year "deadline" for decommissioning was entirely aspirational? May 2000 might have been mentioned in the Agreement but it came and went without any decommissioning whatsoever and its absence did not halt the prisoner release programme? Moreover, Trimble himself incurred the wrath of some traditional Conservative supporters in the House of Commons when he failed to join them at Third Reading in opposing what became the Sentences Act 1998, precisely because it failed to make the linkage between prisoner releases and decommissioning.

"Look, there were two years for prisoner release, two years for decommissioning, obviously set side by side. The mistake was made by the British government in legislating for prisoner releases that would take place irrespective of the circumstances. Because they were so embarrassed at the thought that they were releasing people

because of a political context, they dressed it up as a
special new remission-type arrangement, and they legis-
lated in such a way that gave them no leverage at all.
That was a huge mistake. Now we blamed Mowlam for
it but I'm not sure if the responsibility shouldn't be
placed elsewhere." With Blair himself? "Yes."

I want to leave this subject. However, it seems to me
that Trimble has made a very telling point which goes to
the heart of my still-nagging doubts and confusion both
about the decommissioning requirement in the Agreement itself and, in particular, about his actual stand on
the issue. He says the Agreement is not a big legal
document. But isn't that the nub of the matter? It is in
these vital respects much more a politicians' draft.
Lawyers would have had no difficulty producing a
document which explicitly tied together decommissioning, prisoner releases and Sinn Fein's entry into government had they required to do so. But Trimble was
acting and deciding as a politician rather than as a lawyer. Isn't the fact of the matter that he left it vague and
imprecise because he knew he wouldn't otherwise reach
political agreement? And is it possible that, had he won
the 1998 election with a more comfortable majority, he
would have given decommissioning less priority than he
was otherwise forced to do by the internal unionist
arithmetic at Stormont?

That to me would seem to make sense of the ambiguity. But Trimble is insistent I've got this wrong: "Oh no,

no. Obviously I wanted to get an agreement, I wanted to get a situation that brought unionists in from the margins to the centre. But there was an even bigger prize there because if there was a genuine transition taking place amongst republicans from violence towards democratic politics, then you had the prospect of actually settling once and for all the instability that there had been in Northern Ireland. But if you're going to get them down that path, you know . . . I've complained about the process being 'all carrot and no stick', and I've complained about there not being enough 'push as well as pull'. That's not to say that I don't recognise that there has to be a pull as well."

In other words, he was distrustful while wanting to believe the republican leadership was for real? "I wanted a transitional period. Even if Gerry Adams and Martin McGuinness were absolutely genuine and totally wanted to do this, there was no guarantee that they would succeed. So there was absolutely no point saying, 'Because I've looked these men in the eye and I know they want to do this, therefore I'm quite content.' There was no point doing that because their people might not have wanted to do it. I was not in any event convinced of their good faith in doing it. While I saw there was the prospect of a transition, and that if that transition was achieved it would be a good thing, I was not of the view that republicanism was an entirely willing participant in the transition. They'd partly got into this situation as a result of the security force pressures that were on them. They were travelling down a path that was deeply repugnant to a lot of republicans because it meant slaughtering their sacred cows at every stage along the way. So there was no point in me buying into the pose that 'they really do want peace and therefore everything in the garden's rosy'. I knew that there would have to be a constant struggle. It's taken longer than I expected, yes, but I expected that there would be something like this and I thought that once it started down this road, unionism had the stickability to see it through, and I'm sorry about the fact that a significant number of unionists lacked the stomach for doing what was necessary."

Does he think people sufficiently recognised his achievement in actually delivering the Ulster Unionist Party in the first place? "Well, this goes back to my Private Secretary's comment about the way in which the Irish government look at things. You know, their view is so skewed that they understand nothing about the nature of unionism, so the achievements you're referring to — they're something they expected to happen. Coming back to October 2003 — and you have written about what the British government did to me there. . . . I mean they and the Irish government got into the habit of assuming that, no matter how difficult the situation was, somehow I would manage to pull some rabbit out of the hat and everything would be okay. They never really actually had any gut feeling for the political situation I was dealing with."

One other problem Trimble had, which helped undermine him greatly, I think, was that — while he saw the Belfast Agreement as "a settlement" and a line in the sand over the IRA's challenge to the Northern Ireland state — Sinn Féin characterised it as "a process" pushing remorselessly toward a united Ireland. And, of course, a great many unionists were prepared to believe Adams rather than Trimble.

He readily recognises the truth of that. "Absolutely, absolutely. This is epitomised by that great comment by Adams after the UUC decision to endorse the Agreement: 'Well done, David.' He said that you know there are those unionists who don't realise, in terms of this and of virtually everything that happens, that republicans find it laughably easy to wind up and manipulate unionists."

What was the effect of Adams's words, and what did Trimble think when he heard them? "Oh, I knew exactly what he was doing. I knew it was done deliberately, that this was him winding up unionism. . . . It also has to be said that Adams would not have been able to get all the concessions that republicans have made past his own people were it not for the howls of outrage from unionists."

Trimble has complained in particular about the Irish government's lack of awareness of unionist sensibilities. Presumably he had that in even larger measure from a republican leadership which affected at least to believe that unionists were merely clients of a British government which could command their compliance?

"They always have that, they approach things in much that same light and the consequence of that is that they tend not to understand or to try to understand the political dynamic within unionism. I mean, in the past they didn't bother. It has to be said that for quite some time now republicans have been making efforts to try and find out how unionists tick."

But on that question of the Agreement as "settlement" or as "process": some of the loyalist politicians certainly entered the negotiations acutely conscious of the possibility that unionism could be required to concede a great deal to reach an accommodation with nationalism only to discover that republicans regarded any outcome as the departure point for a further negotiation and still more concessions. And some I think entertained the idea that in return for a generous deal — and in order to overcome the predictable opposition of the hardliners on their own side — unionists should seek to stipulate that any subsequent change in Northern Ireland's constitutional position should require something more than a simple majority. Did that ever become an issue? Not for Trimble: "I don't think — I never have thought — that there was ever any prospect whatsoever of there being a majority in favour of a united Ireland. I don't think that's ever going to happen, ever, ever."

So it wasn't worth bothering about? "I may be completely wrong about that but if I am I'll never see it. Why expend energy on something that's just completely irrelevant?" he replies laughing. Yet there is a serious point here surely. The Belfast Agreement for example represented the triumph of John Hume's argument that majoritarianism does not work in a divided society. In consequence, Trimble and Seamus Mallon required a majority of unionists and a majority of nationalists to elect them First and Deputy First Minister. If dual consent is required for the formation of a regional administration within the United Kingdom, is it not arguable that a higher threshold than a simple majority should be required to effect a change of sovereignty? And even as a matter of practical politics, does Trimble think a simple majority in a Northern Ireland referendum would provide a workable basis to take Northern Ireland out of the United Kingdom and into a unitary Irish state?

He says he thinks "this is possibly why the Irish put in what they did, that there would have to be double referendum before there's a united Ireland with votes in both the six and twenty-six counties". But would a bare majority actually be enough to effect a successful change of sovereignty? "Unfortunately you do have the democratic principle which says in theory you ought to," he reminds me before lighting on my reference to the world of "practical" politics: "You said 'practical'. On the practicalities obviously not. I presume this is why some SDLP people have said — and interestingly some in Sinn Féin — that if there was a change in sovereignty it wouldn't affect the existence of the institutions of Northern Ireland as a unit and that the local administration established by the Belfast Agreement would continue as before. All it would mean would be instead of sending MPs to Westminster you'd send them to the Dáil. Now none of that's in the Agreement and I don't see that it in any way logically follows from the Agreement. But they have said that, and I presume they have said it as their own way of acknowledging the point that you make. As I say it is my view this will never happen, and I don't think there will be any change in sovereignty."

In fact, rather than the Republic assuming responsibility for the North, Trimble ventures: "I think what is happening, has been happening for some time and will continue to happen, is that the Irish Republic will get closer and closer to the United Kingdom. That has been happening for some time but I think it's going to happen further in the future. I don't suppose that the Irish will return to the pre-1921 Union. But they'll get very close to the British." Why so? "There are so many factors, there's the shared language, the shared culture, the shared history, the shared economy, the shared peoples, the closeness, the movement of people. You've got a situation where — if you just take passenger numbers, flights, London/Dublin, London/Belfast — many more people go London/Dublin than go London/Belfast."

Given all this closeness, is there not in fact an argument for some voluntary sharing of sovereignty, some sort of confederal arrangement within these islands?

Trimble's answer is true to the letter of his unionist beliefs but surprises me nonetheless: "Again, the British state will never go down that path in formal constitutional terms. But it's getting close to that path in practical arrangements, in practical working."

So the boundaries between Britain and Ireland, nationalist Ireland and unionist Ulster, are becoming more and more blurred, less and less meaningful and relevant all the time? "They're blurring all the time but the people I see who are threatened by this are Irish nationalists."

Ignoring the threatening and sticking with the spirit of closeness, I wonder how far boundaries have blurred. Could he comfortably now consider himself "a citizen of these islands"? But I should have known it was a stupid question, at least to put to him. "Well, I am," he cheerfully affirms. "Everybody is actually because the famous provision in Section 2 of the Ireland Act 1949 says that the twenty-six counties are not a foreign country. So in a sense the British government has never fully accepted that the Republic of Ireland is really foreign. After all, are we not all part of the British Isles?"

Chapter Four

Losing the RUC

O F ALL THE MYSTERIES OF THE Trimble leadership arguably the greatest still surrounds his and his party's approach to the appointment of the Patten Commission to reform the Royal Ulster Constabulary.

Policing went to the heart of the nationalist and republican agenda for radical change and reform in the Northern Ireland state. For unionists likewise it was the touchstone for everything they valued and believed under nationalist and republican attack.

Nationalists and republicans had long sought to "internationalise" the Northern Ireland situation, and had enjoyed considerable success — particularly following the first IRA ceasefire in 1994 — even before Trimble assumed the UUP leadership.

For years before the Anglo-Irish Agreement in 1985 Trimble's predecessor Jim Molyneaux had taken great delight rising in the House of Commons to invite the British Prime Minister of the day to confirm "that the affairs of Northern Ireland are for the people there and

this House alone". And for years successive prime ministers had obligingly confirmed that this was indeed the
case. Yet even Molyneaux in the end bowed to the
changing reality to the extent that colleagues prevailed
upon him to visit the Clinton White House where he
had a meeting with Vice President Al Gore. And of
course by the time Senator Mitchell was asked to chair
the talks that would lead to the Belfast Agreement most
of the parties were almost eager to claim the idea of a
neutral outsider presiding as their own.

Even so, could Trimble not see that by agreeing to
the appointment of an international commission on the
vexed question of policing he was almost certainly inviting calamity?

"No. I mean how clear was it in April '98 that Patten
would take the form it did?" he counters. "We were actually using the language in April '98 about there being
a Royal Commission on policing. And the proposal for
policing was not terribly clear on 10 April 1998, in its
detail anyway. There was an awful lot of opacity there."

But there was nothing opaque about a document produced months earlier in which Mo Mowlam invited the
views of the parties on the possible appointment of an
international commission to examine the issue. Surely he
knew that the minute the concept was introduced by the
British Secretary of State it would immediately take legs?

He insists not: "But the phrase 'Royal Commission'
was also being used to us. Even if it was clearly to be

international, that wouldn't have excited the same controversy. The fact of having an international element to it would not have excited me to the extent you might have expected. As you say, like it or not we'd already got a degree of internationalism in terms of what was happening in Northern Ireland."

But he must have known from its terms of reference that this commission was going to address the key issues of symbolism, from the RUC's cap badge to its "Royal" title. And since the whole purpose was to gain nationalist acceptance of the police, he must also have realised that unionists could only be the losers on these issues?

"That's right, but commissions don't decide. A commission comes in and makes a report with recommendations. I found it quite astonishing when it later became clear that the British Government got itself into a position where the commission's report was treated as Holy Writ. That is quite foreign to the British way of doing things and it was not signalled at any point beforehand that we were going to have that situation. In fact, I doubt if it was even in the British Government's mind until it came under pressure on the issue in the post-Patten period and this business of treating Patten as the only route. So a commission would only make recommendations and to a large extent one knew that there was going to be an issue about policing, there was no doubt about that. But one saw the political aspect of that issue as being post-Patten, post the report."

I wonder if that was at all realistic. Given the conten-
tious nature of the subject under review, and the hugely
beneficial political consequences both the British and
Irish governments hoped would flow from it, wasn't it
inevitable that the Patten Report would instantly acquire
tremendous moral and political force?

"There was no doubt that a lot of people in London
and Dublin would have approached the issue of the policing arrangements for Northern Ireland from political
positions, with their minds determined largely by the
political positions that they would adopt. And we know
that the nationalists, republicans and the Irish Government would all have come very strong against the RUC.
So was an international group a bad idea in that context?
Was it a bad idea to have a group of people who would
look at this from a technical point of view as policing
experts, rather than coming at it as politicians with a
whole lot of axes to grind?"

Was Chris Patten a policing expert? "No, but there
were policing experts there. I'm talking about the concept. . . . I mean you can't keep writing what happened
back into before it happened. When you approach
things you approach them as they're evolving into a different idea, to the concept of a commission with people
drawn from around the world as well as from Northern
Ireland without knowing the exact nature of the commission, without knowing who any of the appointees
were going to be. Then is it such a bad idea to have peo-

ple who are going to come and presumably be experts
on policing and who would come with an expertise and
an appropriate background? Is that such a bad idea because it might be a way of getting away from all of the
political agendas that people would have? There was
that possibility. Now it didn't work out that way. Why
did the appointments to the commission involve a number of people who were simply not good people? Why
was it that our man on Patten defected to the other side
at some point very early on."

Who was "his" man on the commission, I ask, knowing that we are heading into highly disputed territory?
"A certain Mr Peter Smith, formerly an Honorary Secretary of the Ulster Unionist Council."

I put it back to Trimble that Smith has always been
absolutely clear that he never understood or regarded
himself as the UUP's nominee and would not have accepted his appointment on that basis. Trimble is insistent: "But he was. The truth of the matter is, we were
asked to nominate someone." Formally, as a party?
"Yeah, the British Government asked us for a name.
Now it was not part and parcel of . . . you do not find it
saying in the Agreement that the commission will con-
sist of the following nominees." So Trimble mentioned
Smith thinking that he was a unionist and likely to be
solid from their point of view? "Well I said to Ken
Maginnis, 'I've been asked for a name, who would be a
good person?' and Ken came back and said, 'P.D. Smith

Esquire would be a good man.' And I knew Peter, I'd known him for a long time, knew of his somewhat liberal disposition. But he was also someone who had been involved in unionist politics way back and more recently in association with Robert McCartney. The name seemed not inappropriate to me and we then gave that name to the Government and he was then appointed. It then subsequently appears that where I am at fault in this is in not taking more direct responsibility for the issue. During the talks I left the policing issue to Ken. Ken would deal direct with Jonathan Powell on any policing issue that arose. There's a limit to the number of things you can do and you can look at. Now Ken had successes but he will tell you that he should have been in more regular contact with Smith. But he wasn't and so Smith may have been left with the view that he was a free agent. Even so . . ."

Even so? Was it not extraordinary that the Ulster Unionist Party thought it had appointed its own man to such a critically important position but nobody bothered to consult or tell the individual concerned?

Trimble counters: "I thought that someone who was a former Honorary Secretary of the Ulster Unionist Party would not have seen himself as completely independent." But does he accept that his party actually made no attempt to ascertain what Smith's views on policing might be? "If Ken hadn't spoken to him before giving his name to me then the answer to that is 'yes'. Ken will say that he thinks that he should have been in closer contact with him."

But in fact, as I understand it, Mr (now Lord) Maginnis does not say anything of the sort. To the contrary, my understanding is that Maginnis did not attempt to speak to Smith because he felt it might not be appropriate to approach him as an independent, and explicitly non-party, member of an international commission. Trimble insists that his recollection is very different. But plainly not wishing to open another avenue of dispute with a close colleague he turns his fire on Patten.

"We should have been in closer contact with Patten, and here a large part of the fault lies with Patten because Patten did say to Ken and I when we had that dinner in the restaurant in the Strand in London and we discussed a number of things. When we came to the symbolic issues at the end it was clear there was a minefield there. And Patten said to Ken and me that he would come back to us when it got to the final stages of preparing the report to road-test ideas with us."

I put it to Trimble that long, long before his dinner with Patten he had had more than one clear indication that on the question of the symbolism, the RUC cap, badge and title, etc., the argument was already lost and that these were among the first items binned by the Commission as it set about its task.

But he rejects this. "No, no, no. Nobody indicated to me or hinted to me that there was going to be a total

whitewash. I would have lived with some changes providing there was an element of balance in the changes
and that there was some degree of fairness. I think the
community would have lived with that. But it came as a
shock and only became clear at the end that there was a
total whitewash, that everything had gone. No, it wasn't
clear until the end that we were going to lose everything
on the symbolic front."

Trimble then moves on to the surprisingly large part
of the Patten recommendations with which he actually
had no problem whatsoever. "You see on the substantive front, and this again is something I remind people
about time and again, on the substantive front those
who wanted to abolish the RUC, those who wanted to
Balkanise the force, those who wanted to create 'two-tier
policing' lost out completely. The substance of the
Patten report is the bulk of the RUC's own Fundamental
Review, its own plan as to how it makes the necessary
adjustments to take an anti-terrorist force back to being a
normal police force again. Again I have to say this, that I
think some unionists do unionism a huge disservice
when they talk about the RUC being abolished or it's
being destroyed. That's not true."

Well, the title of the Royal Ulster Constabulary was
passed into the legislative history books, ironically on
the morning of 12 July 2000 as the Commons gave the
Policing Bill its Third Reading. But, counters Trimble:

"It's the same men wearing much the same uniform enforcing exactly the same law."

So for all the furore, it wasn't really such a big loss after all? Interestingly, Trimble doesn't immediately deny this proposition. "Look, we're here dealing with New Labour, dealing with people who think that re-branding is the normal thing to do. We're dealing with governments of the kind which, you know, when they decided there was a problem with the Ulster Defence Regiment decided the way to solve the problem was to re-name it the Royal Irish Regiment. We're dealing too with legislation already on the statute book, passed by the New Labour government, incorporating the police force, the Harbour Police and so on into something called the Northern Ireland Police Service. The name is already understood pre-Patten."

The title of the police force, however, remained the Royal Ulster Constabulary pre-Patten. And it seems to me that Mo Mowlam's first foray into legislation on this subject should if anything have alerted Trimble and the unionists to the fact that the Labour government probably did not consider the RUC title sacrosanct. Yet for all that he allows the name "Police Service of Northern Ireland" was already in the public domain, Trimble exploded in fury when Patten finally abandoned the "Royal" title?

"What annoyed me wasn't just that, what annoyed me was not just that we had a complete whitewash on the symbolic issues, but the whole manner and style of the report. The complete and deliberate insensitivity in the failure to acknowledge the achievements and sacrifice of the RUC, and the lack of any serious discussion of the options. Again and again Patten proceeds by bald assertion."

Yet Trimble says that on the big structural things, presumably the things that really mattered, his opponents lost. The force wasn't abolished, the existing members were not put to the humiliation of having to reapply for their jobs, it was all largely as the then Chief Constable Sir Ronnie Flanagan had prescribed?

I know I'm somehow not quite "getting" it. And this again brings me to the point of suggesting that the result in any event could have been very different, and that Trimble could have ensured it was. Sure, as he says, he was dealing with New Labour and its fetish for marketing and re-branding and presentation and all of that. But David Trimble is not Tony Blair, nor is he New Labour. He is the leader of a very conservative Unionist Party which thinks of itself as a party of law-and-order. If he felt that strongly about it — or, which I suspect the more accurate, if he anyway knew his party and supporters would feel that strongly about it — why didn't he tell Blair this was a resigning issue, that if Patten was implemented in full he would bring the whole political project to a halt?

"And with what result?" he demands. What about "saving the RUC" and maybe even, in time, his electoral majority? It is certainly the view of some of his friends that, over and above the whole question of Sinn Féin in government, it was Trimble's perceived failure to go to the wall for the RUC which inflicted the lasting damage which would in turn hand the majority to his DUP rival.

He agrees: "That's probably true and that's exactly what I said the day it came out." So did it never occur to him to make it a resigning issue and tell Blair "up with this I cannot put"?

"Well we made it an issue that we would not go back into the power-sharing administration without there being changes on these issues. We didn't get very much, though funnily enough we did preserve the name. You've got to look and see what is the real name of the police in Northern Ireland. They only use 'PSNI' for operational purposes. The legal name is 'Police Service of Northern Ireland incorporating the Royal Ulster Constabulary'. That is what the law says."

So he doesn't regret not making it a resigning issue actually? "Well, as I have said on other occasions, there are people who have asked me all through this process to make everything a resigning matter because they're so anxious that I should resign as soon as possible. Anyway, what were you going to resign on? Just a purely symbolic issue of a badge or a name — when on so many of the substantive issues the Report was acceptable?"

Trimble makes a valid point about the motivations of some who would have urged him to break on this issue.

But I suspect he knows why I'm pressing this. For all his public fury (and, dare I say it, much public rudeness) over Patten, his answers reinforce my suspicion that he actually never felt about the RUC issue in quite the same way as the unionist rank and file; that, though he was undoubtedly conscious of the political difficulty it spelt for him, he was looking to what Tony Blair likes to call "the big picture" and reasoning that this was pain necessary to the process of political change. Is there something in this?

"Which is the view the police took," he replies. "When you look at the situation post-Patten and you calculate whether you're going to destroy the process over this issue. . . . To be in a position where the Chief Constable, the Police Federation, as far as one can tell the serving officers themselves, are prepared to acquiesce in the changes. To then destroy the political process by taking a harder line over policing than the police themselves take would to some people at least seem to be rather quixotic. Now that's not to say that I wasn't aware of the damage that this would do and I was really angry at the stupidity of Patten and the Patten commission. . . . It's the argument Eoghan Harris made afterwards, 'The fighting's been over the bike, you've got the bike so at least let them have some stickers on it' . . . that having won on the substance one knew that there was going to be some movement on the symbols. That's why I said to Patten, to make it clear to him, 'you can get the substance right but if you go wrong on the symbols the whole thing could go up the chute'."

Yet here we are in 2004 and life goes on, policing goes on, the SDLP has led nationalist opinion in the way he and the two governments wanted, and nothing actually, on that front at any rate, went up the chute at all.

"Well politically it has been because the difficulties that the Agreement suffered in terms of acceptability amongst unionists in that period have been conditioned as much by that as anything else. Our electoral problems are as much, and probably more, to do with the hurt in the policing family. The leadership of the police and the Police Federation, and ostensibly the senior officers, acquiesced. But in their guts they felt bad about it, and especially those who took early retirement, they and their families felt bitter about it. And there is absolutely no doubt that on the doorsteps, particularly in 2001, we were getting more hassle over policing than over Sinn Féin. In fact, when I say hassle I mean more bitterness."

On his own personal balance sheet, then, if that is so, it might be said that Trimble's management of this was pretty disastrous?

This is painful territory. "Well, we had a huge problem. I mean we could have kept closer to Smith, we could have kept more contact with Patten. But I'm not accepting the blame for that because Patten didn't come back to us and that's the problem there. We gave Patten clear warning that he had to be careful about some of this. We weren't opposed to change but the change had to be done in an acceptable way. And instead we got something that wiped out all the symbols and then was, if anything, quite offensive in the way it handled the past. In the drafting of Patten, the way it was presented, there wasn't just a failure to recognise the service and the sacrifice, it was dismissive of it. So I don't accept responsibility for that; that is clearly the fault of the Patten Commission and then there's also a great responsibility on a British Government that accepts the thing lock, stock and barrel and doesn't make adjustments. Now Peter Mandelson realised there was a need to do something and Blair goes along with Mandelson when he tries to do something. But then Blair loses heart in it and caves in and after Mandelson is out of office a lot of the changes are reversed. So I mean this is something which has to be shared around. But there is no doubt that it caused us more trouble than it should have."

DAVID TRIMBLE'S POLITICAL HERO is Sir James Craig, and that fact too has long reinforced my suspicion that Trimble may have had a much more sophisticated approach to the question of policing than it would have been possible to confide to the unionist electorate.

Trimble has referred in the past to Craig's pact with Michael Collins in which they envisaged a situation where Protestants would police Protestant areas and Catholics would likewise police their own districts. One of the unresolved issues arising from Patten concerns recruitment to the Police Service of Northern Ireland's part time reserve. And one of the key elements in Trimble's failed negotiation with Gerry Adams in October 2003 concerned the timetable for the devolution of policing and justice powers to the Northern Ireland Assembly. Was Trimble drawing on Craig/Collins and thinking of a similar solution to the problem of policing today's divided communities in the North?

"No, I think what Craig did with regard to reserve constabulary. . . . In the Craig/Collins pact it was probably just a tactical manoeuvre, and certainly not something done on principle. I mean what he'd actually agreed to was, in terms of the 'B Specials' [the Ulster Special Constabulary, set up in 1920 to counter the IRA], promising that Protestant 'B Specials' would be used in Protestant areas and that Catholic 'B Specials' would be recruited to support the police in the Catholic areas. He did also agree that they would try to recruit one third Catholics in the police force, and was aided in that by the fact that nearly a fifth of the policemen who had transferred from the Royal Irish Constabulary to the RUC were Catholic."

Yeah . . . so is he to some degree drawing on Craig/Collins for a modern-day solution? "No. The principle of him being prepared to negotiate with Collins and to come to arrangements with Collins, dealing with sensitive areas and how he deals with them. . . . He deals with the response to the technical situation. I would never try to blow the dust off an arrangement of 1922 and say we'll do exactly that in 2002, no. Yet I drew comfort from Craig's actions for the principle of trying to proceed with agreement or acquiescence from nationalists."

Yet winning republican support for the PSNI is plainly going to call for new thinking, and a realistic response to Sinn Féin's insistence that community policing as referred to in Patten must mean policing of republican communities by a police service recognisable as coming from those communities. Catholic police for Catholic districts. Isn't that going to be the reality?

"No I think that's not the way to do it, the way to put it. Part of the new reality is a police force that draws its recruits from the whole of society, and which has an appropriate percentage of Catholics in its ranks, and is a force that the society as a whole is comfortable with. That doesn't mean if you have nine per cent of the populace disabled you have to have nine per cent disabled in the police, it's not that sort of 'representativeness'."

I understand that. But "representativeness" to Sinn Féin will certainly mean republicans in the police force? "The first point is that yes there will have to be Catholics in it, yes its going to be a force that society as a whole is comfortable dealing with. And I see that as being a single force operating in Northern Ireland enforcing the same law everywhere in Northern Ireland. That means that when people approach a policeman in the street there will be a fair chance they're approaching a Catho-

lic and if there's a half dozen policemen in the street
then the probability is that two or three of them will be
Catholic. But it's not a Catholic force for Catholic re-
gions. That's certainly not what I had in mind."

But if you were a republican . . .? "If republicans
have given up violence, and are going to pursue a
united Ireland but do so lawfully, which means respect-
ing the status quo until the status quo changes, then I
don't see a problem."

But would he have a problem if it were proposed to
lift the bar on people convicted for terrorist offences
serving as members of the PSNI? "This is something to
be treated very, very carefully and I think in principle
there is a problem with that concept. We have a position
at the moment whereby people who've got convictions
are excluded and that has to remain, that has to remain."

OK. But other people will have been recruited to the
IRA since the second ceasefire who have never been convicted of any offence. What about them? "They continue
to recruit in fairly small numbers but the people who we
regard as IRA activists now are much smaller in number
than was the position in 1994, and is declining rapidly."

But the sons and daughters of leading, well-known
figures previously engaged in physical force republicanism . . . ? "Well let me get round to the point I was going
to make. People with criminal convictions are excluded.
But with regard to people who were in the IRA during
the terrorist campaign . . . there were lots of people there

who've never had convictions, so what's the position there? And there will be people today who don't have criminal convictions who are supporters of the republican movement, who vote for Sinn Féin in elections, so what is the position there? If they're identified as people who are supporters of a movement which is now operating by purely peaceful or democratic means, on what basis do you find an objection?"

So a Special Branch report, for example, on an applicant, Citizen X, confirms he or she has no convictions while identifying X as the son or daughter of Citizen Y who served time for offences committed when he was commander of the local Provisional IRA unit. . . . That doesn't provide a basis to object?

"Say you've got X who is active in Sinn Féin or whatever, but has no previous convictions, is not known to be engaged in any criminal or anti-social behaviour and he or she joins the police. Then he or she will have to drop their political activity. On what basis do you make an objection in that situation? The problem I would see comes with people who don't have records but who had been known to the police as having been active during the time of the terrorist campaign. That is a problem. But then the longer this goes on the less that's likely to be a problem simply because they'll be getting too old."

Some might think Trimble too sanguine and that, on past form, republicans will eventually persuade the British government to scrap the criminal records because they were actually only incurred in the context of a "political" conflict. Indeed, some nationalist commentators are absolutely certain that is the situation we will have to get to in any event. How would he respond to that development?

"Well, they may say that but I don't accept it and I think that the British government has given commitments about not doing that. We would be very foolish to go down that path. There is a concern clearly about the part-time reserve, and it's fairly obvious what Patten envisaged, that the part-time reserve would be recruited on a local basis. And so consequently it will reflect the balance of the population and it would be a way for example in south Armagh whereby we can recruit people who identify with the republican community to be there with the uniform."

But could this not prove the way to cantonisation? "No, it's not. Any part-time reserve is going to have a local recruitment basis no matter what you're dealing with. A part-time reserve is pretty small beer in the scheme of policing but it is nonetheless necessary that you keep the proper controls to make sure that the individuals you are recruiting to the part-time reserve are fit and proper persons to have the powers of a constable. That is important and that has to be maintained. I understand that to be the government's position. Now we're here with the problem of 'will the government stick to its position or do something foolish somehow and manage to create anxiety and all the rest of it?' There are all sorts of problems around this which again is why the part-time service is something that will have to be watched carefully. But a part-time reserve is only an element of the police. The thing you've got to do is to make sure that the individuals who are recruited are fit and proper persons to be a constable."

One problem will be that many unionists will think anyone who supports Sinn Féin almost by definition not a fit person, and that republicans will only contemplate joining the police in order somehow to subvert the force or the state itself. Does Trimble not share that fear to some degree at least?

"Well, this is why it's so important that the concept of consent is internalised and that what we mean when we talk about acting like peaceful and democratic parties is really understood. That it means that you operate in terms of the status quo until the status quo changes, so you uphold the laws of the status quo until the status quo changes. And that is how it should be and if people are operating on that basis then there isn't a problem. Now, if we have a situation where people are paying lip-service to that status quo and are then trying to have a means to undermine it . . . there is the danger that past mistakes will be repeated. But you know, life is full of problems and dangers."

Chapter Five

Dealing with Dublin

W HILE MUCH OF THE POLITICAL TALK had long centred on the need for a partnership administration
in Northern Ireland, any durable settlement would first
require a historical rapprochement between unionist
Ulster and nationalist Ireland, which in essence meant
between Trimble's party and the Irish government of the
day. When did Trimble first realise he could do serious
business with Bertie Ahern?

He promptly reminds me this would not necessarily
have been his obvious preference. "I have to say first of
all that we had had hopes of being able to do something
with the coalition government that was there beforehand led by John Bruton. He is a person for whom I had
considerable respect. He's rightly referred to as 'honest
John' Bruton and I'm quite sure that he was. One thing I
found quite frustrating was that we arranged a couple of
private meetings and on each occasion the meetings
were leaked to the press. I'm sure not by John Bruton —
but they were leaked in a way that was not helpful to me

at all. And I got the impression that, while John was anxious to do something, there were elements in the Irish system — which we rightly or wrongly attributed to the Department of Foreign Affairs (DFA) — who were trying to prevent things from happening. Now round about the same time as part of this business — which followed through right from my very first days as leader, and my commitment to going and meeting and speaking to people and doing so in such a way as to get rid of all the shackles that unionists had in the past, in some cases voluntarily, put upon themselves — I had on one occasion agreed to meet all the opposition parties in Dublin. That meant meeting Mr Ahern for the first time.

"It was a very surreal meeting. I think there were three of us and we met a panel of three from Fianna Fáil, one of whom was Mary O'Rourke, who sat and glowered and never said a word the whole meeting. Just sat and glowered at us. Now it may have been just our over-sensitivity but I really had the feeling that she had difficulty with us being in the same room. As I say, that may be just a question of our perception.

"Mr Ahern had been given a brief which he read out, straight from the script, in a rather hurried manner. I have to say at that first meeting I was distinctly unimpressed. It seemed to me that the sub-text of what was being said was that 'we're the biggest party down here, you're the biggest party up there, why don't we get together and divvy up the place between us?' That may not have been what was intended but it struck me as an incredibly naïve approach and failed simply to recognise that we were unionist in a sense which was not a matter of tactics but reflected a real sense of identity and a real desire to continue as part, as we always have been part, of the United Kingdom."

An inauspicious start, then, to his dialogue with Bertie Ahern. But the situation was very different after Trimble met Taoiseach Ahern at the Sheraton Belgravia Hotel on 20 November 1997. "Again that was slightly disconcerting. It was supposed to be a private meeting and by the time it had finished somebody was looking out the first floor window and said RTÉ had just arrived. But that didn't spoil the occasion. I can't actually point to anything that was specifically said or done. We opened up some of our ideas for, not just a North–South arrangement, but something on a British Isles basis, what became the British–Irish Council — and we got the very distinct impression that, while nothing was agreed, the Irish government was in business for the sort of things that we had in mind."

Understandably, given the passage of time, Trimble's recollection of this meeting seems somewhat hazy. But it was more than an impression he took away from that encounter. Indeed, such was the excitement generated on both sides that *The Irish Times* reported it the following day in terms of a significant breakthrough in the relationship between the Ulster Unionists and the Fianna Fáil-led government in Dublin which had significantly improved the prospects for a political agreement on the North.

Trimble affirms: "My impression of Bertie is of a pragmatist. The impression that I got rightly or wrongly was that he doesn't have much historical baggage." So — despite the fact that Padraig Pearse was reportedly his idol, and that according to one biographer Ahern only joined Fianna Fáil rather than Irish Labour because of his republicanism — Trimble didn't actually get the impression that he was dealing with a committed or driven republican? "That's what I mean by saying that he is a pragmatist. There were plenty of people who said to me, 'Oh, you can't trust him, he's just a wheeler-dealer and this is his background in trade unionism, it's just a matter of cutting a deal.' I know that there have been tensions obviously, he has got a different view-point to represent and I don't expect him to agree with me all the time and I don't expect him to approach issues in the same way that I would. And of course he has people in the DFA who are driven by an ideological viewpoint and that sometimes causes problems. But I do have to say that in the dealings I've subsequently had with him, I've never had the sense or an occasion which I can point to and say he deliberately let me down. Having said that about not having let me down or anything, can I draw a contrast? The very first time we went into the administration after the Mitchell Review . . . a few months previously President Clinton in a speech said he didn't see why unionists didn't go ahead and set up the administration and if republicans didn't keep their promises then the unionists could walk away from it. He said that quite clearly. Yet when the time came — when we had done precisely what Clinton had urged and the republicans had let us down and we were urging suspension on the British government — Clinton opposed the suspension. Indeed, we have reason to believe that even after the suspension order had been made, over the telephone that evening, he spoke to Blair and asked if he could lift the suspension. Which seemed to me to be inconsistent with what Clinton said earlier. Now we didn't have any equivalent behaviour from Ahern. I never asked Ahern for assurances on the matter. I didn't expect him to welcome the situation that then arose. It was perfectly obvious to me after we set up the administration in December 1999 that the republicans were banking on the assumption that 'once it's set up people will then be tied in and they'll never suspend, that unionists won't want to suspend and governments won't support them if they do'. Now I knew that was their position. I fully expected a Dublin government to incline to that viewpoint and I was relying on the promises that I'd got from Peter Mandelson and Blair. That's why I would put the behaviour of Ahern at that time in a different context in my mind to that of Clinton."

Because he knew Ahern would be against him, would at the very least have to go through the motions of opposing the suspension? "I knew there would be a problem there. And I think that while he had to represent a position then and on other occasions which was not the same as ours, he understood too the factors behind what we were doing."

So, how early on in his talks with Ahern did Trimble realise that the problem of Articles 2 and 3 of the Irish Constitution, which laid claim to the territory of Northern Ireland, would in fact prove very easy to resolve? He says: "That's difficult to know because of course John Major's negotiations over the Framework Documents had come onto the reefs over Articles 2 and 3 because they hadn't been able to get language from the Irish government that would clearly do the business on that. And it wasn't really until an advanced stage in the negotiations that we saw text. Until then we were getting general assurances from the British that the Irish would make the necessary changes. But we didn't actually see text until the end. It wasn't something that bothered me because I think my view was that the Irish knew this was something that was going to have to change, and that for us it was an absolute irreducible requirement that there was that change. I fully expected when the time came that that change would come. My general impression of the approach of the Irish state to this issue was that they felt honour-bound to support Northern nationalism but that it was a matter of honour rather than a matter of a strong desire to see a united Ireland.

Essentially what the Irish state wanted was an honourable compromise that left the present basic structure of a Northern Ireland, you know, a six-county Northern Ireland and a twenty-six-county Irish Republic, but did so in terms that they felt that their historic debt to Northern nationalism was now paid and they'd be able to go their own ways and live their lives and all the rest of it. My impression is the Irish state was not in fact seeking a united Ireland either now or in the foreseeable future. What they wanted was to be able to feel that they had paid their debt to Northern nationalists."

This assessment is wholly consistent with the view advanced throughout the period by one senior Irish player, that in order to win the unionists would have to lose on a series of issues because the real object at the end of the day was to reconcile the Catholic community in Northern Ireland to the reality of ongoing union with Britain. However Trimble adds a qualification to this: "When I say that's the position of the Irish state, that's an overall view. It doesn't conceal that within the Irish establishment there are people who are driven by ideology, for whom it does represent 'the fourth green field'. Rightly or wrongly, I'd put Sean O hUiginn in that category, and the decision to despatch him to Washington and to leave the conduct of Northern matters within the DFA to someone who was a bit more pragmatic, seemed to me a clear signal."

This is interesting and important detail. In a straight swap, O hUiginn became Ireland's Ambassador to Washington while Dermot Gallagher became Head of the DFA's Anglo-Irish Division before going on to head the Office of the Taoiseach and finally becoming Secretary General of the Department. Some tried at the time to explain the move as simply part of the process of change within the civil service. However, that did not silence the speculation that Gallagher had been drafted in at a point where Dublin's need was for a smoother relationship with the unionists. O hUiginn had acquired a reputation for being "very green" and as a formidable negotiator with the British. Even among his British detractors there was more than a sneaking regard for O hUiginn and the brilliance of his analysis. And while he undoubtedly fought every nationalist corner, it was acknowledged in Whitehall that he was first and foremost a constitutionalist who fully subscribed to the Trimble view that the republican transition from terror to democracy required an eventual end point. But no matter. O hUiginn had acquired "bogey man" status with the unionists and, whether by accident or design, the incoming Gallagher was a very different sort of operator who had actually managed to cultivate personal friendships with a number of leading unionists over the years. So Trimble welcomed Gallagher's appointment?

"Well, it was more a welcome for Mr O hUiginn's departure," he laughs. This reluctance prompts me to ask if this change in personnel actually marked any shift at all in the basic Irish disposition. Wasn't there at work here a classic unionist tendency to pick on somebody and demonise them? Wasn't Trimble doing in respect of O hUiginn and the DFA in Dublin what he also did with the Northern Ireland Office in Belfast, blaming Mo Mowlam for decisions probably taken over her head and using that as an excuse to bypass her and deal direct with Blair?

"No," he insists, "I think there's substance to this. You say 'demonising'. No, I think there is actually substance to this, that there are people in the Northern Ireland office then and now who take a view about policy which is not precisely the same as the view taken on policy in London. Government is not monolithic, there are always different elements, different perceptions and views of the situation within it. And it seems to me that there is a very clear distinction. We judged by what was happening that the change within the DFA was significant. We likewise found that when Paddy Teahon was in the Taoiseach's office there was an openness and a straightforward desire to achieve progress which we felt wasn't reflected to the same degree when Paddy Teahon retired."

Some of David Trimble's friends recall that his attitude to Dermot Gallagher was not always so warm. However this is his account and he at least allows that his and his party's perceptions of key players may or not have been right. And friends and admirers of the man certainly think Trimble and the unionists were wrong to fall for, and then perpetuate, this stereotype of Sean O hUiginn as ideologically driven. Others too — whether because they had greater direct knowledge of the Irish system, or because their dealings with Dublin were of a different order — would subscribe to the view that one of O hUiginn's key contributions was actually to defuse much of the theology attending the republican movement's transition into politics.

As one key insider of the time puts it: "The idea that this was all about theology is very wide of the mark. You have to remember what was being attempted at the time, and also that republicans came into this process with a huge distrust of Dublin and its relationship with the Brits. If the republicans were to be kept on board, particularly during that long last desolate winter of the Major government, there were certain essentials. You had to show that there was independence to Irish foreign policy. Sean would have taken it as a matter of course that you couldn't cheat terrorists and that therefore there was no room for bullshit, no place for lying to them, that we needed to build their confidence in our independence and in our competence. But this wasn't about ideology at all. This was rational business. Our job was to deliver the republicans and we all would have shared the view that it was for the Brits to deliver the unionists."

While conceding that O hUiginn's famous tempera-
ment would have informed unionist perceptions, this
source ventures that O hUiginn was in fact happy to
leave when he did because he knew, in terms of the Irish
government's dealings with unionists, he had in fact become a liability. However, he agrees that this timely and
politically advantageous change in personnel did not
mark any significant change in the basic disposition of
Irish foreign policy. And he adds: "This was all much
more complex than the unionists seem to think. The important thing to remember is that when O hUiginn went,
the show had been kept on the road through a very difficult period, people were beginning to talk to each
other, and the outlines of a deal were in view. It wasn't
just by happy coincidence that everything fell into place
after Bertie Ahern became Taoiseach in 1997."

But the task of completing the process did fall to
Ahern, and Trimble would come to the view that Bertie
was the man for the moment and probably in fact the
only leader who really could have done the deal? "I
don't think any of his predecessors could have, and I
don't think any of his predecessors would have put the
effort in that he did in the last week of negotiations. We
all remember Blair flying in from London. But a lot of
people seem to forget that for Ahern coming to Belfast at
that time was a huge step, particularly with his mother
dying. He could very easily and very understandably
have said, 'No, for personal reasons I can't come.' But he

came and again there was an openness and a flexibility. We would not have got that agreement and understanding on how to manage the arrangements with regard to the North–South Ministerial Council [NSMC] on the Wednesday night without both Ahern and Teahon being in the room.

"It became clear to us later that they had started off with a different idea about how to do things and when we put our alternative ideas as to how to do it in front of them they were quick enough to see the merit in what we were saying, and flexible enough to move on that. It also became clear to us that they had a previous approach which they had discussed with the SDLP, and that there were people within the Irish camp saying, 'Oh, we agreed with the SDLP what is going to happen here, so we can't change that and have an arrangement with the unionists which is different to what we've agreed with the SDLP.' And what was being sought there was something that could be represented by nationalists as being a victory over unionists. Instead, what we had when we finished that negotiation was something which achieved the aims and objectives of the Irish in terms of putting in place the NSMC and ensuring that there would be serious content, without there being an element of imposition on unionists. From our point of view it did the business without either party feeling in any way upset by it. But there had been elements within the Irish camp and northern nationalists who wanted, as it were, a tribal victory as well. Indeed, they had to close down the negotiation, end the session then in order to go and sort this out within the Irish delegation and between them and northern nationalists. So that to me was a significant element."

What about the man himself? Does Trimble like Ahern? Is he somebody he would have a drink with, be happy to spend an evening in his company? "We really got on very well and he has a habit when we're in Dublin for meetings of wanting to have a private chat beforehand, before the delegations formally meet. He and I would go into a room together and just sit there for ten or fifteen minutes and chat. He relishes doing the business privately and then we'd go out and have the meeting, and there would also be a little sort of personal element in the conversation and he clearly prefers to work that way."

And how important was this personal rapport given that Trimble's subsequent relationship with Deputy First Minister Seamus Mallon would prove so problematic?

"I don't like to personalise these things too much, though there is a personal element within it. Before I come to personalities, there is an important point to make. This was our greatest disappointment in terms of the Agreement, apart from the obvious problems with decommissioning, prisoner releases and all the rest of it. We had stretched ourselves to get an agreement on the basis that within the compulsory coalition there would be a voluntary coalition and that ourselves and the SDLP, being the two centre parties, would effectively run things together. That had been my leitmotif during the negotiations and the meetings that we had with the SDLP, to repeat our desire to operate in that way."

A voluntary coalition? "When I say a voluntary coalition within the compulsory one, I meant that we would work together closely in order to run things, yes. We would each have alongside our difficult wings, the DUP on our side, Sinn Féin on their side, who would be locked within the process. Inclusivity achieved this by locking them in so they would not be running pure oppositional campaigns right from the outset. But within this compulsory coalition, we, the SDLP and Ulster Unionists, would have the majority within the executive. Indeed, one of the reasons why I agreed to having First and Deputy First Ministers, which was not our idea at all, was when it was pointed out to me that this was a way in which the SDLP and Ulster Unionists could each get an extra ministerial post."

So why didn't it happen? What went wrong with this plan? "Somewhere within the SDLP, and I don't know where, a strategic decision was taken that, rather than operate in that way, rather than position themselves closely with us, they were going to position themselves close to Sinn Féin. And rather than work with us in a whole-hearted way they would continue as it were to promote themselves as being more effective nationalists at the business of beating unionists. They regarded the post-Agreement discussions as a way of showing that they were tougher nationalists than Sinn Féin and that they could extract more from unionists and push unionists further. That seemed to me to run absolutely contrary to the basic assumption of the whole Agreement, namely that we were going to put a co-operative arrangement in place, where we would work together, sharing with each other, instead of approaching the issues with a mindset of 'I'm going to do my best to screw you'.

"One of the reasons I found it difficult working with Seamus is that in almost everything that he did he was looking for party advantage. Again, in one of the early meetings I remember a senior official saying to me that I ought to treat everything 'as a wee negotiation', and that 'that's the way to handle Seamus'. I found that extremely difficult because I thought we were dealing with policy issues and that we should deal with them on their merits. To deal with them always as a negotiation between two parties and thus to be settled on a party political basis, on a basis of party advantage — 'I'll give you a bit of advantage for your party in this issue and you give me a bit on that' — and always to do everything as a negotiation on a party basis rather than deal with policy issues on their merits is something that seemed to be quite foreign to what we were supposed to be doing."

Seamus Mallon of course would offer a very different perspective on his often stormy relationship with

Trimble. But given that things did not work as Trimble had expected, this presumably made his happier relationship with Ahern all the more important. Sinn Féin and the SDLP would naturally look to him to back their position on any issue. But was Trimble likewise able to turn to the Taoiseach and have him impose some limit, some constraint on them?

Trimble recalls one famous occasion when he says this is precisely what did happen: "This was during that awfully protracted business we had in December '98 in trying to sort out the departments, and it was clear that this was being done on a party basis. Rather than looking at it from the point of view of the well-being of the service, as to what should the departments be, what should they cover — it became an awful haggling matter and went on into the early hours of the morning. Then at a very early hour Dermot Gallagher came into the building and went to the SDLP and told them, 'Come on, it's time to sort it out, time to settle.'

Does Trimble regret now that John Hume chose not to serve as Deputy First Minister? "How can you tell? I presume with regard to this strategic decision taken by the SDLP to position themselves closer to Sinn Féin than to us, that he must at some point have been involved in or party to that decision. So if that is the case then it's too facile to say a different personality would make all the difference."

And how did Trimble assess Ahern's attitude toward Sinn Féin and the IRA? "I never felt that he was going to be easy on republican violence and I think that has been borne out by the way in which the Irish state has worked effectively in dealing with people like the Real IRA. So I never thought there was going to be any sort of weakness there. With regard to achieving decommissioning and so on, again I got the impression that this was something that they too were committed to achieving. There were, however, points at which they would be driven purely by self-interest. The Garda McCabe case is one point. Another was where Ahern made this point about the Irish Constitution and that republicans couldn't be involved in any form of coalition in the Irish government while there was still a private army in existence. There were of course a lot of unionists who . . ."

Who resented what they saw as a double standard, I offer. Didn't he? "I was going to say a lot of unionists felt this was a little bit off, that they were telling us to form an administration with them while saying it couldn't happen in the Republic. And it was a contrast. But look, we were only getting involved with Sinn Féin on the basis that there was a transition that would bring about the end of the private army. We never went into the administration on the basis that we would still be there if there was no transition and that there would always be a republican private army that was armed and threatening. We only went into the administration on the basis that this was a transition in which the arms would disappear and the private army would disappear."

So Trimble was not implicitly accepting an Irish double standard — a suggestion that he had reason to be doing something in the North that would not be acceptable in the south? "No, it's not as if we're going to say, 'Well, you will be doing that and that is how things will be because of your different circumstances.' That's not as I understood it because we were only acting on the basis that there would be a transition, and at the end of that transition we would be in exactly the same position as Ahern was. So to see Ahern take that position, I felt actually strengthened us. That was the position to which we were moving and wishing to move and the fact that he supports the projected end state carries with it implicit support for the transition."

With hindsight, might Trimble not have been better to insist that the entry point for Sinn Féin in government should have been the same in both jurisdictions? If Ahern had been required to adjudicate on Sinn Féin's fitness for office in the Republic would this not have driven the search for acts of completion and probably secured them? "This brings us to the big question we had to face in November '99, because that's the point at which such considerations would come into play. Would we have been better off saying to the republicans, 'You've got to do the business in terms of decommissioning first before inclusion'? Now, historically, the fact that we decided to be more flexible tactically, forming the administration first whilst still sticking to the principle of decommissioning . . . the question is, were we right in taking the position we did? The situation then was that we had been supported on the need for decommissioning. We had a certain amount of support from others, but that support had fallen away by the autumn of '99, and we were then seen as obstructing the implementation of the Agreement. And by obstructing the implementation of the Agreement we were also obstructing our own objectives. Decommissioning was something that we wanted to achieve but there were other things that we wanted to achieve at well. And we had to say, 'Here we are, our support has fallen away, we are now, if not completely isolated, heading towards a position where we will be isolated — and furthermore, we are stultifying our own project, so we're not actually going to achieve any benefit.' So we would lose the efforts we'd made over the previous number of years to achieve progress, whereas if we modify our tactics while still sticking to the principle, then we create a different situation. We took that position rightly or wrongly then. I still think it was the right thing to do. It would be nice of course, like so many other things, if somehow the thing could be re-run and the circumstances were different. But in the circumstance we were in we didn't have much choice."

This is important on two counts. First, Trimble acquits Ahern of the charge of operating a double standard over

Sinn Féin's fitness to hold office. And he also acquits him of any suggestion of compromising the integrity of Ireland's own democracy by urging unionists to enter government with Sinn Féin in the North without first forcing the IRA to stand down? Isn't he more than a little bit generous to the Taoiseach? And needlessly so, given that another member of the Irish government reportedly rationalised the perceived double standard by reference to the North continuing as a "failed political entity"?

Trimble is as ever dogged in defence of his political friends: "I think Ahern supported — and still does support — the concept that there be a transition, and that the end state we're heading toward is a situation where there isn't a private army and people are behaving normally, and I cannot see anything that he has said to depart from that. For example, the Joint Declaration in April 2003 with its demand for an end to paramilitarism. That in no way indicates that he has moved from the basic objective of achieving that end state."

Moving beyond Bertie, does Trimble now regret calling the Republic monocultural? "Let's put this in context. I've said on a number of occasions that one of the reasons why we got an Agreement is because there has been a change in the way in which the Irish Republic perceives itself. You know, way back in the late sixties, early seventies when all this problem blew up, I think most people in the Irish Republic thought in traditional nationalist republican terms. But the entry into the European Union and the various social and economic changes which have taken place there have led to an extent to people re-inventing themselves as a modern Irish nation within the Europe Union. In that context, old-fashioned territorial nationalism is no longer appropriate. And so there is a sense in which there has been change and people in the Irish Republic see themselves as having changed. However, having said that, there is still very largely a single culture, a culture of Irishness in which respect is given to a language, to a particular view of history, to various sporting activities and all the rest of it. By contrast with that, the United Kingdom is not monocultural, even if we don't take into account the migration that's taken place from Africa or from the Indian subcontinent. The different perception of people, the different nationalisms that exist, English, Scottish, Welsh, within the United Kingdom, means that there is a pluralism that is there even before we bring into account the very substantial migration that's taken place. There is a contrast and bear in mind I'm contrasting Ireland with the United Kingdom."

Yes, I was about to venture that many in the Republic would have been particularly offended at being lectured on monoculturalism by a man famed for leading the Orangemen down the Garvaghy Road, an MP from a society noted for its diversity but hardly, even now, for its inclusivity? Trimble accepts and understands that this attack on the Republic caused dismay even among his supporters and admirers there: "I think you're right, that was part of it. This was the famous occasion when the language that was used in the speech that circulated was a little bit over the top. The text had already been circulated. I saw the night before the UUC annual meeting as I was looking at it . . . 'pathetic sectarian' I think was the term that was in the text and my pen went straight through it. And when I saw the gentleman who had been drafting the text next morning, I said, 'You've got to change this.' And he replied, 'Too late, it's already gone out to the press.'"

Again this episode will strike people as evidence of an at times extraordinary amateurishness in the management and conduct of Ulster Unionist Party business. As Jack Straw once famously conceded about Downing Street's first "dodgy dossier" on Iraqi weapons, it was in fact a complete Horlicks? Trimble concedes in respect of the particular phrase used while maintaining, "there is a substance underlying this". But I'm keen to give him further opportunity to redeem himself. Does he like the Republic? He resists, telling that his only visits over 30 years have been fleeting and for business only, before adding: "But I have to say I don't feel drawn to spending more time there. If I have a choice as you can see from the pattern of my life I visit the rest of the multicultural society that I am part of."

Chapter Six

Blair Necessities;
The Adams Handshake

DRIVING EVERYTHING, OF COURSE, was David Trimble's need for a harmonious relationship with a new British Prime Minister who enjoyed a massive majority in the House of Commons. Many of those triumphant Labour MPs from the 1997 intake had also learned their politics in the 1960s and would be assumed to be instinctively anti-unionist or, at any rate, pro-nationalist. Did Trimble see himself in a position of weakness from the outset in his dealings with Tony Blair?

"No. One of the things we needed to do was get him engaged on Northern Ireland. There was no obvious reason why he would take himself to Northern Ireland in the week or so after the general election. So why did he do it? Part of the reason of course was that the cease-fires and the talks had put Northern Ireland at the heart of British politics in a way that it hadn't been before. But also during the previous winter we had been in touch with Blair, sending papers and suggestions to his office, effectively saying, 'There is the possibility of an agreement here that could settle the position once and for all.'"

Despite the assumption that he was dependent on unionist votes as his Commons majority disappeared, Trimble says that John Major had been keen to carry things forward and to conclude an agreement before leaving office in 1997. Trimble, however, didn't regard that as a serious option: "The Conservatives had a legacy going back to Thatcher and the Anglo-Irish Agreement, so there was a slightly emotional element about not trusting the Conservatives. There was also a bit of me feeling uneasy with Major, which I confess I did."

In what way? "Well, I was never quite sure with Major where he was grounded. People sometimes make the same comment about Blair but I think it applies with greater strength to Major. Anyway, weeks after the Belfast Agreement I bumped into Michael Ancram, the former Conservative Minister of State at the Northern Ireland Office. He smiled and offered his congratulations. And I said, 'Thanks, but I got a better deal from Tony Blair than I would have got from you.' And I still think that was the case."

So, while some might have imagined that the Provisionals and Sinn Féin had held back on Major, thinking to fare better under a New Labour government, Trimble also preferred to wait and deal with the man already deemed certain of victory as Major's government staggered through the mire of alleged sleaze and incompetence?

"When I said that to Ancram, that was my view, that we had got a better deal from Blair than we would have from the Conservatives." But why was that? "Because I think Blair wasn't tied to the Tory inheritance, the Downing Street Declaration, the Anglo-Irish Agreement and so on, because he was seeing things in simpler terms." Then he adds the rider: "Now do bear in mind that this was my view within a couple of weeks of the Agreement, and that when we saw how the government threw away negotiating cards it had over prisoner releases, then the deal wasn't as good as I thought it was. What I was saying to Ancram reflected my belief that we could achieve IRA decommissioning quite easily because government had levers, you know, the two-year programme for prisoner releases, the two-year period for decommissioning, they were clearly paralleled and we hoped there would be linkage between them."

To what extent did Trimble think Blair was acting in response to some imperative of British state policy? "I'm sure the primary thing was responding to an imperative. There was always an imperative to manage Northern Ireland, now there was the opportunity to settle it. There may also have been a personal element as well."

The "personal" Trimble thinks may have had to do with Blair's family ties to Northern Ireland, and holidays spent in Donegal. But on the question of his personal relationship? Molyneaux was thought to have got too close to Major. The same would subsequently be said about Trimble in relation to Blair. Is this maybe a fate that awaits any unionist leader?

"Any regional party like the UUP needs to deal with the government of the day. Some wondered why I wasn't lining up with the Conservatives and leading the charge against Blair. In many respects I'd be quite comfortable doing that and indeed that [an alliance between the UUP and the Conservatives] is what I'd like to see happen. But then, it's not 1912 or 1914 when we were part of a great national party, which was actually called The Unionist Party, and fighting the Liberals over their desire to fracture the United Kingdom. And working with the prime minister of the day does mean establishing a relationship. So you're right to say there is that danger." However, he adds: "Unionists and much of the Northern Ireland media have a flawed perception of London. It's partly a chip on their shoulder, partly a belief that London is always plotting to get rid of them. Which is quite wrong. Unionists keep believing the nationalist propaganda to this effect and, of course, seeing this, the nationalists keep piling it on. Then too they fail to take account of the situation as it seems to government, they don't realise governments' difficulties and the pressures on government."

Even allowing for all of that, some unionist critics would say Trimble was actually in awe of Blair. Was he?

Trimble recalls Blair saying "that I could be a difficult person to deal with" before listing retrospectively some of the many difficulties he presented to the Prime Minister. Recalling that earlier question about why he didn't make the RUC a resigning issue, Trimble invites us: "Track it back. When I stopped the sequence [of statements confirming a new agreement for the restoration of the Assembly] in October 2003 — Blair wanted it to proceed — I stopped it in its tracks. When in February 2000 I lodged my letter of resignation as First Minister with the Assembly Speaker in order to bring matters to a head, I tried to speak to Blair shortly beforehand. He was unavailable and Jonathan Powell asked if there was any chance of persuading me to change my mind. I said, 'No, that's why I waited to the last minute before informing you.' And I would have said the same thing to Blair. And again later in 2000, when we were contemplating going back into government, we held back to get movement on issues like flags and the RUC title. We had a meeting of the UUC convened as per the government's timetable and we cancelled it until we got what we wanted from Blair. I don't think I was tame at all in my dealings with him."

The only "wobble" Trimble admits to was over a negotiation conducted at Downing Street on 14 May 1999 about yet another possible "sequence" of moves on all sides to permit the restoration of the Assembly. This resulted in an *Irish Times* report that he appeared to have "lost the run of himself" and concluded a deal which

Bertie Ahern visibly believed Trimble would be unable to sell to his own party.

David Trimble's account of that day's events is wholly different. "I left Downing Street actually determined nothing was going to happen. And you're right, Downing Street tried to bounce me by alerting the press to expect a major announcement the following Saturday afternoon. I went to my Assembly group meeting and circulated the proposal which was then formally rejected. In a fit of pique, Downing Street then set another deadline of 30 June and indicated that they would run the d'Hondt formulae to form a new executive whatever happened. Well, that deadline was bypassed. And then later on in July when the government proceeded to carry out its threat to try and force the appointment of an administration, I kept my Assembly members away from Stormont, and confined them to party headquarters, to make absolutely clear that it wasn't going to happen."

Trimble might have added that he also persuaded Tony Blair to postpone the scheduled Assembly elections in 2003 not once, but twice, on the grounds that the absence of republican "acts of completion" meant there was no guarantee an election would result in a restoration of devolved government. But then Blair denied him at the third call. Worse still from Trimble's perspective, we now know that Blair had promised Sinn Féin the election would proceed by the end of November 2003 at the latest even before Trimble embarked on his final, ill-fated negotiation with Gerry Adams. Did Blair betray him on that occasion?

Trimble's response is measured: "I think he made a mistake. Why? I think partly because we had had a good summer on the streets and he felt republican efforts to achieve that should be recognised and rewarded. We were a bit miffed at that, because the republicans hadn't done it on their own and why weren't our efforts to be rewarded? I also assume he probably believed it would be all right because, you know, 'We're going to have the republicans deliver the rest of the goods.' And then he was so far involved and committed he couldn't turn back and he still thought, 'It will still be all right because Trimble always manages to deliver somehow or other.' Then when the election results were coming in and it was clear that this time I wasn't going to be able to pull it off, that the DUP would have more votes and more seats, we were most amused to be getting these agonised phone calls from Downing Street saying, 'This is terrible, what are we going to do?' To which our response was pretty blunt. The criticism that I make of the Prime Minister is this — that he has a tendency to believe that his energy, charm and goodwill can solve all problems. And this rushes him into positions sometimes where the outcome isn't as good as it might be. I think Blair made a mistake in making the promises he did to the republicans. The question is whether I made a mistake by re-engaging with the republicans that autumn or whether I should have held back."

It seems to me that Trimble is surprisingly generous to Blair, not least because Bertie Ahern subsequently made clear he knew there remained a problem over the issue of "transparency" about the IRA's third act of decommissioning. Indeed, the Taoiseach told the Dáil he had not been disposed to travel to Belfast. And yet knowing there was a problem, and unable to communicate with General John de Chastelain, the head of the International Decommissioning Commission, Blair and Ahern allowed the planned sequence to kick-off with the presumably irreversible announcement of the election date. They cut him adrift, didn't they?

Trimble accepts that "Ahern's instincts were better" and that the Prime Minister and Taoiseach had had it in their power to halt the planned process until they were able to satisfy themselves that General de Chastelain's report on the decommissioning would be satisfactory. "Absolutely, Blair would have been much better following Ahern's advice because it is clear, I think, that Ahern was saying, 'I don't think this is a good idea, I don't think this is going to work.'"

Trimble also reckons that Blair's heart scare the previous day may have been a factor in his determination to proceed with a high-profile event and so dispel speculation about his health.

Whatever Downing Street's calculations about Blair's image requirements, the reality seems clear enough — they cut Trimble adrift and left him to face his electorate on back of a failure. Isn't it the case that David Trimble was undone when he could no longer hold Blair to his previously declared standard on the necessary acts of paramilitary completion?

Painful as it might be, yet oddly with no hint of bitterness, Trimble finally assents: "That's right."

So Blair was subsequently wrong, then, to blame the republicans for the UUP's electoral defeat in that the British government at least shared in the responsibility for it? "Oh yes, absolutely, there's no doubt about that," comes a reply which will attend and inform the historical verdict on Tony Blair's Irish peace mission if it ultimately fails.

What about the man himself? Opinion is still divided as to whether Blair is a supreme political leader driven by unshakeable core beliefs or an actor/manager driven by nothing more than the need always to win the next election. Which is he? "Well, he's both obviously," Trimble replies. "There are some core things there but there is also the actor/manager, and the magpie element too, always looking out for bright ideas. But the core isn't a clear view, for example, about the nature of the public services and how to sort them out. He's not ideologically driven as to the means of doing that, he doesn't actually have a clear ideology." And what did Trimble think of that day for no soundbites when Blair felt 'the hand of history' upon him? "A bit contrived," he allows, his understatement echoed in his laughter. More importantly, how does he think history will judge Blair in terms of his contribution to the resolution of the Northern Ireland problem?

"I actually take the view that what we did in the talks is the basis of the solution to what people call 'the Northern Ireland problem'. That is what I said to Adams the very first time we actually spoke. I told him that in my opinion this Agreement, the basic principles that are in this Agreement, give or take a little bit, is where the outcome is going to be. Because Blair was involved in bringing about the Agreement, then he is going to be seen as having made a huge contribution. But history is also going to record George Mitchell's closing comment about getting the Agreement being one thing while implementing it was going to be just as difficult. That is going to be seen as equally true. The judgement that people are going to make about Blair, about how Blair handled the implementation, is going to be a bit more variable. I suspect that when people get the chance to see some of the actual papers, it's going to be seen that Mo Mowlam was a lightning rod for decisions that he took, that many of those weren't good decisions, that throughout the period of implementation there was a tendency by government to be too solicitous of republicans and too great a willingness on the part of Blair's government to assume that unionism could carry greater weight. So I think that is going to be a judgement that will be made."

Was Blair overly responsive or susceptible to the influence of the Clinton White House? "We engaged with Clinton to try and get him to be more even-handed and we never entirely succeeded in doing so. We got him to get a little bit of balance in his approach, but I think Clinton was always leaning far too much in the Irish republican direction. It might be easy to assume that that was having an influence on Blair, but Blair has continued to have the same sort of approach even post-Clinton. I have sat with senior US officials from the Bush administration who have said to me, 'We can't understand why he isn't tougher in his dealings with republicans.'"

Yet when Blair postponed the Assembly elections in 2003, the Bush State Department appeared onside with Dublin in urging that the elections must proceed. Trimble agrees that "this was the view taken by Richard Haas, the President's personal envoy", while maintaining, "whether it was that of the Bush White House or not I don't know".

This is a matter of considerable curiosity. Of course, no one would have expected President Bush to be familiar with much of the detail of Northern Ireland affairs. But given Blair's expenditure of personal and national resources on behalf of Bush and America in the fight against international terrorism and in Iraq, surely one phone call from Number 10 Downing Street would be enough to have the Americans backing any position Blair wanted on the North?

"My own impression of Bush is that Bush is not going to do anything to embarrass Blair and that Bush feels indebted to Blair. And therefore that would lead one to think if Blair had spoken directly to Bush on this then there almost certainly would be a different approach from the US administration. And it does leave one scratching one's head as to why that did not happen.'"

Well, maybe it didn't happen because while Blair felt obliged to side with Trimble on this issue, at least publicly, it actually suited British policy-makers to have the Americans applying the pressure in the opposite direction. Perhaps in fact this was a very early warning sign that Blair would ultimately let him down on the question of the Assembly election?

"Well, I'm just saying that there are things here which we cannot explain and where one can see that it ought to have been possible for something to happen, it didn't happen, we don't know why it didn't happen, and the one thing I don't like doing in this situation is jumping to conclusions."

RATHER INCREDIBLY, DAVID TRIMBLE and the Ulster Unionists negotiated the Belfast Agreement without ever speaking to Gerry Adams or his colleagues in Sinn Féin. I recall writing that historic weekend that somewhere along the path of a tactical engagement in the talks process, Trimble had obviously made the leap and come to accept Sinn Féin's bona fides. Yet two years later, Trimble was still insisting he had done nothing of the sort. Was it wise for him to have agreed the terms of any deal without first satisfying himself that the IRA cessation was genuine and that the peace process was not in fact a variation of the republican stratagem of "an armalite in one hand and a ballot paper in the other"?

Trimble too recalls our past discussion of this issue. "That's right, that's right. Look. How do I put it? My view was that the republicans were coming into the political process not as a result of having had a road-to-Damascus-type conversion, and a realisation that the violence was wrong and that they really ought to commit themselves to peaceful and democratic means. I did not think that we were dealing with people who had such a conversion. I thought that they were coming into the political process partly as a result of the pressure that was generated by the realisation that their campaign was failing and partly as a result of the attraction of possibly achieving things through politics. So I said that their position, the ceasefire and the movement into politics wasn't a matter of principle but was essentially driven by tactical considerations. That didn't however mean that you should therefore say, 'Oh, these people aren't genuine, so we will ignore them.' Because they were being driven by circumstances, it seemed to me that they could still continue to be driven, and it is my

view looking back at it that I think the republican position has changed. It has changed significantly as a result
of them being in the process. So by admitting them into
the talks, I wasn't regarding them as being a party with
whom I would have to negotiate in order to get agreement. I could see that an agreement could be obtained
without having to negotiate with them because of the
sufficient consensus rule that the talks were operating
under. I was negotiating with the British, the Irish and
the SDLP to get an agreement that would hopefully
achieve my objectives but also at the same time lock the
republicans further into the process and take them further down the process as well. As for our particular position of not actually speaking to them in the building
and all the rest of it, there were tactical elements in that
because we were having to manage our own party, as
well as actually having to manage our own selves."

But did he not feel a bit ridiculous at times, not
speaking? He promptly reminds me this was the least of
his difficulties back then: "I found it very difficult at first
to actually cope with them being in the room. I don't
think we had any illusions about their character, and so
having them in the room was a difficult thing, a very
difficult thing, and even to engage in social pleasantries
was not easy. You're dealing with people who you
know have been responsible, if not personally for plant-
ing bombs and pulling triggers, of having directed a
campaign which planted bombs and pulled triggers and

resulted in hundreds, thousands of deaths having occurred. So that was a difficult thing to deal with, and
one did not feel comfortable."

This of course was why Trimble for so long declined
to shake Gerry Adams by the hand. He famously made
the point that the handshake was to show there was
nothing in the hand and that he could not know that.
"Look, getting to the point of actually talking to them
was a difficult thing and of course what eased that was
when we got the statement that was supposed to be a
statement equivalent to the war being over, you know,
the convoluted sentence that violence must be a thing of
the past, over, done with and gone."

And then, admittedly for just a few brief weeks in
the first instance, he shelved his doubts and sat with
Sinn Féin ministers around the cabinet table. Which of
them by this stage was he most inclined to talk to, which
of them did he actually like? "Well, I don't know
whether I've ever actually engaged in a social conversation. In the early days the conversations were all about
the business we were doing, they weren't personalised.
We had of course the long discussion at Winfield House
during the Mitchell Review, which involved us sitting in
a room speaking, talking about the politics of the situation for hours on end, and I remember the time Adams
digressed at length about how we ought to get to know
each other better, go out and socialise together, spend
weekends together. He kept on talking and I let all this

go on until he came to a suitable gap and I turned round to Martin McGuinness and said, 'You know, Martin, just because you get to know someone better doesn't mean you like them any more.'"

So when did he begin to like them? "Well, I'm not sure . . . I don't . . . I'm choosing my words in this. I don't think one can assume that I do. I don't know that I do," comes the earnest reply. Yet, by September 2003, he finally felt able to shake hands with Adams. Where did the famous handshake take place? Trimble confirms it took place in the former First Minister's office at Stormont. "It was when we were starting the September conversations which eventually led to the aborted sequence in October 2003. Way back in April of that year, after we'd reached the end of that round of unsuccessful talks, Adams and ourselves started to discuss how we might handle the problem of sectarian interfaces during the marching season and over the summer. It seems a little bit strange to go from trying to construct a sequence, failing because republicans haven't come up to the mark, and then having discussions about handling the problem of the interfaces. But we had a whole series of meetings which even got down at some point to talk about individual interfaces and brought people in from local communities. An example is Ardoyne, an area of North Belfast which is difficult, which had management problems for republicans. Reg Empey and Fred Cobain were there with me and Adams had come with a group of people from the

Ardoyne. I think really the purpose of the meeting wasn't so much anything we'd actually agree, it was I think just a matter of getting these people involved and letting them see there was serious commitment and political leadership in terms of getting things sorted out. And it worked. Northern Ireland had its best summer for a decade. It had been a situation where republican violence had just simply disappeared. There were still some punishment beatings taking place but anything that would have had any impact on the unionist community had disappeared. Now I thought that was quite a considerable step forward from Adams. In the spring failing to make a declaration that paramilitary activity was at an end, but working hard during the summer to achieve that, you know, without actually saying it. That seemed to me to go a long way and I know it also impressed Blair as well, so that's the context."

And did the handshake occur quite spontaneously or had he thought about it in advance? "No, I hadn't given it any thought beforehand. I would put it under the category of spontaneous." So, Trimble just extended his hand? "No, Adams extended his hand and I took it." Somehow or other he knew the moment had arrived and this just seemed the right thing to do? "Yeah, I thought it would have been churlish not to in view of what had happened in the summer." Were there witnesses to this event? "No." And did Adams say anything after they had shaken hands? Were they both embarrassed? Was there a little awkwardness? This was quite a moment for the pair of them in highly personal as well as in political terms. Was there maybe a tear in the eye that day? A lump in the throat?

Trimble laughs as he assures me that "there certainly were no tears" before admitting, "There might have been a little bit of an awkwardness and I suppose, yes, there is" — before rushing on to more comfortable terrain. "What I was actually going to say to you, the First Minister's room was obviously unoccupied and consequently we did use it from time to time in order to have meetings. I think actually it quite amused Adams, when we were going to have a meeting, to slip into the First Minister's room. But I remember on one occasion we were going in there to have a chat and we were just sitting down when a ladder appears at one of the windows. Chap gets up on the ladder and he's cleaning the window, so we move to the outer office which the private secretaries would occupy and we were again sitting down and starting the conversation when, bloody hell, another chap with a ladder appears. So we pop back round to the First Minister's room again to see if all's clear. But no, the first window cleaner's still there cleaning the windows and we had to conclude we weren't going to be able to continue this conversation until . . ." So they had a laugh together? "Oh we did, we did, and there were sarcastic comments about the length to which the British state was going to keep tabs on our talks."

Seizing on the serious aspect of that reply, I ask Trimble if he assumes that the British do take steps to monitor his discussions with Adams? He takes us back instead to the American Embassy in London. "We'll go back to the Winfield House talks and the Mitchell Review. It started off in Belfast and most of the meetings conducted there were very bad meetings, very bad-tempered in the republican party, and we responded in kind. Then Mitchell said he wanted to spend some time in London, and we said 'OK', and then Mitchell came back to us and he said that he'd found all the usual places, Lancaster House and the rest, were fully booked up. So what he was going to do was go to a hotel, and we said, 'Oh no, not a hotel, because the press will find out, we'll be besieged by them, we won't have any privacy and it would just be a mess.' Then I thought of Winfield House which I had been in for a reception just a while before. I knew that the redecoration had been completed. I mentioned it to Mitchell and he said, 'No, it's not available yet' and I suggested he go back and check. And he went to look at it. Some of our colleagues wondered if it was wise for us to have an American venue. And I replied that it was probably the only building in London that M15 wouldn't have bugged, because we all know what happened in Lancaster House during the Rhodesian/Zimbabwe talks. Then we went to Winfield House and started the talks and it was just chalk and cheese. It was totally different to Belfast. Instead of being angry and causing rows, the republicans were polite and expressed themselves politely and there was serious conversation. I was curious about this, and then it occurred to me, 'It may not be bugged by MI5 but I'm sure the CIA's got it all taped and the likelihood is that either this is happening or the republicans fear that it might be happening, that summaries of the conversations might be on Bill Clinton's desk the next night after each meeting, and this might very well account for the fact that they've got a very different approach to the talks now'."

One possibly quite different reason, of course, might have been because Mitchell's transfer to London had worked its magic, that they had been obliged to sit down and actually share a civilised meal together. Sure, it might all still have felt terribly stilted and strained, but isn't there a point here? John Hume has talked often about the accident of birth that put people on different sides in the conflict in Northern Ireland. Isn't it also true that the politics and the sectarianism compounded by republican and loyalist terrorism dehumanised people on all sides? People born into the republican tradition and at the coalface of the war inevitably viewed republican activities from a very different perspective, a perspective perhaps reinforced by a feeling that they had been ghettoised and never really treated on an equal basis and at an ordinary human level?

Trimble won't concede much to this at all. "There were elements of that there but that's not what caused the conflict. We now have an attempt by republicans to re-write history, that they were merely fighting for equality and civil rights. No they weren't, they were fighting to destroy our civil rights, they were fighting to impose a united Ireland on the people of Northern Ireland against their will. That's what caused the conflict. There's a huge difference between the civil rights situation and the civil disorder that we had in August 1969, which was on a par with the civil disorder that we had in Belfast in 1935, both in terms of the scale of the rioting and indeed the actual number of fatalities. There's a huge difference between that political agitation and the civil disorder that resulted from political demonstrations, and the creation of a private army that goes to launch a terrorist campaign in order to impose a united Ireland. That is what the war was about, and the fact that republicans are now re-writing history is again another signal that that war is actually over, because they're not now prepared to defend what they did in the terms in which it was done. I think that is hugely significant."

Trimble has said several times that he believes what propelled republicans into politics was the knowledge that their campaign of violence was failing, had failed. Now, there are some conspiracy theorists — and they are not all Irish nationalists — who believe or at any rate suspect that in order to bring republicans to this realisa-

tion, some of the secret agencies of the British state con-
spired and colluded with loyalists in order, as one senior
DUP politician has suggested privately, to "level the
killing field". Is it absolutely inconceivable to Trimble as
an Ulster Unionist leader that the British state could operate in such a way?

"I think in the society that we live in it's inconceivable that the state would behave in such a way and it
remain a secret. Look at what happened with the Span-
ish socialist government's dirty war with ETA. These
agencies are not such efficient bodies that they could run
something like this without traces of it coming out.
What we're dealing with actually is something quite different. It's not the state as such, it's not 'M' sitting in his
plush offices at the side of the Thames, carefully planning how this, that and the other thing's going to happen and being able to conduct it with ruthless efficiency.
That's fiction. You have individual persons who may do
this. I mean that's why the information leaks out from
police stations and army, you know, giving information
about republicans. That's leakage and it's also penetra-
tion, because I'm quite sure the paramilitaries have deliberately tried to insert people into the police and the
army for this purpose. That again is not the state doing
it. Then you've got people who get a bit gung-ho about
what they do and this is certainly a concern with regard
to some of the agencies of the state in running agents. In
turn the whole business about agents becomes incredi-

bly complicated. I mean, if we take this 'Stake Knife' business. Was the person named actually a British agent? Then it was said that his boss, someone who has since died, was also an agent. As one Belfast journalist put it, 'You thought you were going to be a rebel against the British and you were able to join this organisation. But who took the decision on whether to allow you to join? The internal security section of the IRA that was run by British agents. So it was the British state who decided that you'd be able to rebel against them!' Then, I mean, running agents inside an organisation is a highly ambiguous situation and creates all sorts of moral and legal problems. So you've got these situations, there may very well be more than one can of worms that might arise because of the questions of how agents are run. But whether the state as a whole? I'm deeply sceptical about that because I don't think it could be done successfully in a way that some conspiracy theorists suggest. The agencies are not that good."

Chapter Seven

Loyalists

W HAT ABOUT WHAT WE MIGHT call David Trimble's collusion with the loyalist parties to the talks, the Progressive Unionist Party and what was the Ulster Democratic Party, respectively representing the para-military forces of the Ulster Volunteer Force and the Ulster Defence Association? There was a memorable image of Trimble and his colleagues entering the first day of the Mitchell talks flanked on either side by the hard men of loyalism. What was the thinking behind what looked to the outside world to be an intended show of strength? Was this not a pretty crude declaration to the effect that unionism had its own armed wing?

Trimble laughs off any such notion: "No, of course not, not in the slightest. Put this in its context. It's the first day after the 1997 elections, with the situation where the government has invited in Sinn Féin and as a result of that Robert McCartney's United Kingdom Unionist Party and the DUP have left the talks. Now, we were operating on the talks under a ground rule that decisions would be

by unanimity or where there was a 'sufficient consensus'.
Sufficient consensus was defined as a majority of unionists, and a majority of nationalists, a majority being determined by reference to the elections to the Forum in
1996. The Ulster Unionist Party did not get a majority of
the unionist vote. It was the largest single party but it was
not over fifty per cent of the unionists' vote. The DUP and
its allies were fewer in number than the Ulster Unionists,
but we didn't have an overall majority and the element
that would give us a majority was the loyalist parties. So
therefore, when we were going in, looking at that phase
of the talks, we knew that in order for there to be an
agreement, not only it wasn't sufficient for ourselves to be
there, we had to have the loyalist parties with us. That
being the case, the simple calculation meant that we had
to keep them close, and I can't remember from where the
suggestion of all going in together came, but it was a suggestion that could not be turned down because of that
need. There was a sense too of wanting to demonstrate
that we weren't going in to those talks, which were likely
to be seen as quite a big thing — to engage in talks while
Sinn Féin was there — we did want to show that it wasn't
just one or two people sneaking in by themselves, that we
were all going as a group."

But wasn't there also an element of signalling that
they weren't going to be a pushover either? Wasn't there
a certain machismo element to the thing? "Well, I suppose so, putting on a show. But I think what was in my

mind was making clear that we weren't going in in dribs and drabs, apologetically, with our heads down, that this was something we were going into with a very positive attitude.

"There is a little story attached to it. We'd actually intended to go in the previous day and then dissident republicans let off a bomb in Markethill and I realised, 'We can't go in today.' Instead I went down to Markethill and I remember some people shouting at me in the street about not going into talks now 'with these people', you know, the usual failure to distinguish between one republican and another, the assumption that 'they're all the same anyway' that doesn't do unionism any help. At the same time, I said to myself, 'I've had to postpone one day because of Markethill, I'm not postponing more than one day because that looks like weakness.' We had taken a strategic decision to go in, so therefore we go in the next day. And next morning when, in order to get this large group of people together, we're all sort of milling around in the outer car park, my mobile goes. Downing Street switchboard, straight on comes the Prime Minister, and he asks, 'Where are we?' And I said, 'We're in the car park outside the talks, just about to go in.' And I heard the relief on the other side and he said, 'Good, they were telling me that you would never do it.' And he said this was good from the point of view of building confidence. Now that is my dominant recollection of that day."

But can he at least see from a nationalist or republican perspective that he, encircled by these hard men, conveyed what they would consider at least an ambiguity in the attitude of so-called "respectable unionism" toward the loyalist paramilitaries? "Well, that wasn't what was in my mind at the time. But I did see regularly in nationalist newspapers afterwards a sort of feeling, 'Why are they bitching about republicans when blah, blah, blah.' And our answer to that would be that the loyalists, when they declared their ceasefire, did so in more forthright terms, making it clear that they wanted conflict to be at an end.

"The key thing was that the terms of their statement and their ceasefire made it clear that they wanted the conflict to be at an end. We'd never got the same clarity from republicans and, had we got the same, if there had been the same clarity from republicans, and it had been meant by republicans, then a whole lot of the problems would never have arisen. I mean decommissioning was fixed on as a means of trying to get evidence of their intention. The whole argument about how 'They can decommission today and re-commission tomorrow so what's the point of it?'; the whole point of it was as evidence of intention, in a context where people had refused to give clarity of their intention. They kept hinting and getting other people to brief on their behalf, but they never themselves in terms said 'it's over' and if they'd said that then a lot of the difficulties of the last half dozen years would not have occurred."

Indeed, for all that nationalist perception, I in turn put it to Trimble that there are those in the system in Britain and Ireland who might say that, far from embracing the loyalists, the unionist leadership had been far too coy and that maybe — with the benefit of hindsight, having witnessed what Hume was doing with Adams and the evolution there — it would have been better if the established political leadership of unionism had been talking to loyalists more directly and discussing the politics of the evolving situation much earlier?

"Well, I wonder why that is said, because in 1994 the loyalist ceasefire followed a matter of months after the IRA ceasefire, and the willingness of some elements of loyalism to get involved in politics was very clear. So I don't see anything that was lost as a result of such coyness, and I'm not actually sure to what extent there was such coyness anyway in that there were, there have always been, people within the mainstream unionist parties who have kept lines of communication open to loyalists."

Whatever about that, nationalists and republicans have continuing difficulty with what they consider the double-standard applied as between the Provisional IRA and loyalist paramilitaries. Trimble has in part explained that decommissioning assumed greater significance than it might otherwise have done because of ambiguity in republican language about their intentions. I can also understand the argument employed by ministers that, since the loyalist parties are not to be part of an Executive, there is and needs to be a stronger focus on Sinn Féin. But looking back on it now — and indeed looking forward — wasn't this in fact a major weakness in the entire process? And for this reason: it seems to me highly improbable that the IRA, whatever language it deploys, will actually fold its tent and rule itself out for all time and for all purposes, while loyalists remain armed and engaged in continuing violence, or at least the continued threat of violence. Wouldn't it have been better for the health of the entire political project to have tied the loyalists in more directly, perhaps even by specifically linking them to one of the unionist ministerial posts — both as a means of engaging them fully in the political process but also then imposing the same obligations upon the loyalists that were being imposed on republicans?

"The lack of symmetry in terms of political pressures is an obvious point and an obvious problem. The solution, however, is what should have been the solution on the decommissioning issue anyway, namely that the release of prisoners should have been tied to decommissioning, and that would have applied with regard to each particular paramilitary organisation, that it would get its prisoners out pro-rata with decommissioning. And there was, as I have said to you, an implicit link in the Agreement between the two-year decommissioning process and the two-year prisoner release process. The classic and the huge error that was made by government was not ensuring that linkage. And the responsibility for that is unequivocally laid at the door of government."

He says this, yet — as with their divergence on the policing issue — Trimble fell foul of some Conservatives when he refused to join them in opposing the Third Reading of the Sentences Act precisely because the linkage was not there in the legislation. But he continues: "Had they maintained the linkage on that, then the asymmetry would not have occurred, the ambiguities would not have occurred and of course we wouldn't have had the problems of the last half dozen years because then that would have compelled the paramilitaries individually and collectively to make clear their position and to act accordingly. That, I think, was a huge mistake and having made that mistake government then compounded it by handling the paramilitaries constantly with kid gloves. Then that got us into a process that was driven with carrots but no sticks and you see then how the process begins to lose its integrity and begins to lose its credibility with the electorate as a whole."

Many loyalists would say "carrots in plenty for republicans but actually too few altogether for the loyalists"? "That's their perception of the process as the process degraded through the failure of government to police the thing properly. Government was very good in getting the Agreement and most of what is in the Agreement is OK. There are a couple of points of weakness. The real problem with government was that in the implementation of the Agreement the government let its standard slip and having started to do that then found itself in a position where things seemed to be driven by paramilitary pressure. That has been the problem. We've mentioned it before: George Mitchell's comment that implementing the Agreement was going to be just as tough as making the Agreement. Unfortunately, government wasn't tough in that situation."

We obviously can't know as we discuss these matters in the summer of 2004 how the political situation will develop in light of the electoral ascendancy of both the DUP and Sinn Féin. But looking ahead, and to the business of recovering the standards Trimble says government has let slip, would that still require a new engagement with loyalists, a new political project targeted at them, because loyalist alienation does seem to me to be deeply injurious to the overall process and to the task of bringing the two sides together and settling the situation once and for all?

"Over the course of the last year or so government has begun to address the loyalist alienation and there is a pilot project beginning already in the Shankill area of Belfast which will be extended to a number of other areas, focusing on community capacity building, and designed to provide a vehicle for them. Loyalists realise that they don't have political prospects and they're now looking towards local community development and involvement in that as creating a path for them. These pilot projects have grown out of the work of the Loyalist Commission. So some effort is being made there but we still have the asymmetry in that the rewards available, the carrots for loyalists, are less than the carrots that are there in terms of republicans. That's partly a consequence of the electoral process."

Could he explain why loyalists don't have political prospects? "Well, you start with the fact that by and large the unionist electorate will not vote for people who identify themselves as being persons who've been involved in paramilitarism. By and large they will not vote for them. I think it is because of the community's identification of itself with law and order, with being in favour of the state and consequently its organs, the army and police and all the rest of it. And also disgust then at the actual things that loyalists do. Whatever they like to think of themselves, the loyalist paramilitary organisations I think end up appealing to a lot of the worst elements in the unionist community. And some of the people who have been involved in loyalist paramilitarism, are really persons who . . . one only has to mention the Skankill Butchers and things like that . . . you've got people who are, if not psychopaths, then just one step away from it. There are far too many characters like that."

OK, the average Protestant and unionist does not support these people because he or she supports the state and identifies with the agencies of the state. But

Trimble's party has suffered electorally, and these loyalists too are voters. Even given that the loyalist parties themselves have no great prospects, I suppose what I'm driving at is the disaffection within the areas from which they spring, and in which they do enjoy levels of sympathy, if not electoral support. That disaffection is bigger than them and wider than them and represents an acute political problem because it is reflected by large numbers of disenchanted Protestants who no longer vote either for the Ulster Unionists or for the DUP?

"We're dealing with some complex matters here. Turnout in working-class areas has always been lower than turnout in middle-class areas. That's not a phenomenon unique to Northern Ireland, you can find it throughout the United Kingdom, probably throughout the Western world. And in working-class areas you're going to get a higher proportion of people who are distrustful of the whole system, economic system, political system, and will be saying of the politicians 'they're all the same'. It's like the time I was coming over Westminster Bridge on a number 12 bus with the family during the summer shortly after I'd been elected and with little to indicate that I was a respected member of the House of Commons. And as the driver crosses the bridge and pulls in he calls out, 'Next stop, thieves' palace.' So there's a member of the English working class and his view of politics. The same is true in Northern Ireland, but the increasing element of people who are not voting

— and it is something that's been increasing in the last twenty years — are people who actually dislike the sectarianism of politics, and the fact that local politics have a degree of futility about them, haven't been able to do anything really and 'what's the point of getting involved in politics'. That's the additional factor. You've always had a turnoff factor in working-class areas, which is common. Then you've got another factor that's coming into play through increasing disenchantment with the political process, and that's as much affecting the . . . 'middle class' is not the right word . . . the phrase that's been coined is the 'garden centre Prod'. He's working class and middle class as well, who feels the political process either isn't going to achieve things or that the people and the characters in politics don't represent him. So you've got an element of that.

"I think there's another important point to make. In so far as the loyalist paramilitaries have achieved any electoral success, they've achieved it within a particular constituency that's a Belfast working-class vote that historically was a left-of-centre vote, very Old Labour. And of course it's no coincidence that Gusty Spence's brother was at one time of his life a member of the Communist Party, and the Communist Party in Belfast achieved its highest vote outside Clydeside — and for exactly the same reasons as it achieved its vote in Clydeside. So you've got an element there that loyalist paramilitaries were able to tap into but it's limited and it's declining."

All of that makes sense. But I want to take Trimble back to the point on which we started this discussion because it seems to me it is too easy for establishment unionists to rationalise the problem of loyalist disaffection, and that they cannot actually afford to do so because that disaffection poses a serious challenge to any attempt to establish a stable and harmonious Northern Ireland. Given that he marched into the talks with these guys around him and recognising that he needed them; given also, I presume, that he accepts that people like Gusty Spence and David Ervine and David Adams and Gary McMichael of the loyalist parties were in their own terms grappling with some pretty tough and sophisticated judgements in moving the people they were associated with down this path, and on Trimble's side rather than Paisley's; does he feel in any sense that he failed in that relationship to build them sufficiently and to ensure that that section of loyalism felt it too was experiencing a political reward for having supported the Agreement? It seems to me they shared his analysis, were sick of Paisleyism, felt that was the road to nowhere, and supported Trimble in seeking an accommodation with nationalists and republicans, only to find themselves thereafter pretty much reduced to the margins and feeling that there really wasn't much in it for them or the people they represented?

"Yeah, well they should have joined my party. Unfortunately, that's the reality of it, because going out and having their own party in competition to both the Ulster Unionist Party and the Democratic Unionist Party meant that they were then in competition with us. They were seeking then their own electoral support and that was limited. There was no way I could have increased their electoral support. If they were to gain and to share in the fruits of office, then they could have joined the party or indeed coalesced with my party. In the way, for example, that at times both the PUP and the UDA's representatives have done so in City Hall in Belfast. So the example was there, they preferred to go their own way."

Was this coalition option something he ever discussed with them? "No I did not myself at any stage raise that with them. I can't exclude the possibility of others having done so, but they preferred to go their own way."

And while nobody seems much these days to be talking about the future of the Ulster Unionist Party, because the political focus at least for the present is elsewhere, is such a coming together of the loyalist Progressive Unionist Party and the Ulster Unionists still a possibility? Indeed, is that a possible dimension to a future UUP recovery? David Trimble is not saying No. "The political situation in Northern Ireland is still in flux and so you can't rule anything out on these matters. Who knows where we're going to get to."

BEYOND THE POSSIBLE FAILURE of loyalist expectations, many would argue that the entire process to which Trimble has devoted himself has failed because — far from producing the voluntary coalition within the compulsory coalition driven from the centre by the Ulster Unionists and the SDLP — it has ended in fact with the erosion of the centre and the triumph of the political extremes, with sectarianism even more entrenched on both sides of the fence. What does he say to that?

"First I'm not sure if that's an accurate picture. Yes there is a tendency to talk about Sinn Féin and DUP as the extremes, but these extremes today, 2004, do not stand where they stood in 1998, let alone 1994. So there's been huge movement in the extremes, indeed I suppose I'd even say that my greatest triumph was the fact that I have got the DUP to adopt all my policies. As we sit here this summer the DUP has been putting out statement after statement which could have been written by myself. It's very difficult to find where the differences lie in terms of the principles being espoused and of course they are trying to do a deal and they're trying to get that last little bit that we have been trying to get over the last number of months. Whether they succeed or not, I do not know. So to that extent I contest the charge, because these extremes are not where they were.

"The other thing is that none of this was knowable in 1998. There was no way of knowing, for example, that it would not be possible for us to co-operate with the

SDLP in the way that we had hoped. We did not and could not have known the particular approach that the SDLP would take or the evolution that would come within the DUP within the last couple of years, because bear in mind the DUP remained in simple total negativity until after 2001. Only after their failure in the general election in 2001 do they then decide to track us and grab some of the centre ground vote. None of these things were knowable. I've told the story before about sitting with Daphne a couple of weeks before the event, describing where I thought we could get an agreement but with no guarantee it's going to work. The party might reject it, the electorate might reject it and, if that's so, one's political career would come to an abrupt end. And I've mentioned before Daphne's response that she thought that we'd probably get just enough support to keep going at each stage. But one of the things that was in my mind putting these prospects there was that I could see there was a chance of getting an agreement. The cautious approach, safety first, would probably have not pressed on in the way that I did because too much of it was uncertain and unknowable. But I did press on because, while so much of it was uncertain and unknowable, I said to myself, 'Look, there is a chance that this could work and nobody's going to know unless we try. But if I play safety first, that's okay for me, maybe okay for the party, but from the point of view of the community as a whole, I will have deprived them of the chance which they may take or they may not take. But if I don't myself move forward then I deprive them of that chance.' And that seemed to me to be a strong argument that I had to seriously consider. That doesn't mean there was an obligation on me to be suicidal. But I had to seriously consider whether there was a realistic prospect or any prospect of this succeeding, in which case it seemed to be my obligation to pursue that chance and give people the opportunity. And I would again, you know, despite the fact that it hasn't worked out just exactly the way one had hoped at that time, one hoped on the evening of 10 April 1998. Nonetheless, I think so many things have happened for the better that justify the decision that was taken then. That £800 million private-sector investment in Belfast is an obvious consequence of what has been achieved. Not only have we secured our constitutional position within the United Kingdom but our position is more peaceful. The Independent Monitoring Commission reported just one PIRA murder in the first period of its operation. So, yes, I think the changes and benefits have been huge."

Chapter Eight

Losing the Election

TRIMBLE HAS EXPLAINED HIS POLITICAL mission while saying there was no obligation on him to be suicidal or to sacrifice his party. He obviously meant it in the political sense. However, this was a sharp reminder that life has been pretty rough at times for the Member of Parliament for Upper Bann. How gruelling has it been, really? There were physical restraints placed upon his ability to travel around his own constituency, at least in unionist areas. There were the harrowing scenes from his election count when he held his Westminster seat in 2001 and police had to manhandle him and Daphne away from enraged Paisleyites. And what about the impact on his family? To the outside world, Daphne Trimble may appear a tough and assured political wife. But she is also a wife and a mother. They have children to raise and care for. Did it ever occur to David and Daphne Trimble that perhaps the game wasn't worth the candle and that the best thing might be to pack them up and get them out of there altogether?

The reply is an emphatic "no" accompanied by a quick rehearsal of the virtues of Northern Ireland's education system. But given all the angst and political poison, did it really never occur to them that maybe this wasn't the way to be bringing up the kids? Trimble explains how peace was secured by some measure of isolationism. "Because I remained in the house in Lisburn outside of the constituency, and because the children kept a fairly low profile and I kept a fairly low profile in Lisburn, my eldest two got virtually to the end of their school career before anybody twigged who they were. Whether the younger two have been getting hassle, I don't know, I can't see any sign of it. The ethos of the school was entirely one that would be supportive of the approach one has taken in politics. There's that side of it and, again, the atmosphere and the connections in the Church have been entirely supportive. So my family have been largely insulated from it. We had a number of unpleasant occasions when people came and picketed the house in Lisburn. But if I had been living in the constituency that would have been much worse. Yes, there are stressful bits of it and the scenes that you mentioned at the count in 2001 are visible but actually I've had worse scenes on many occasions at which the cameras weren't present. So, there are problems there. And the scenes in Portadown aren't really driven by anti-Agreement feeling, that has been driven by Drumcree feeling. Drumcree has been a driver there more than anything else. And it was an issue which anti-Agreement politicians came in to exploit but that's a different matter."

Unionist politicians down through the years have obviously lived their lives at risk from republican assassins. Did it ever occur to Trimble that the greater danger to him following the Agreement might come from disaffected loyalists? "I've never officially been advised by the police of a risk of that nature, never officially been advised. I was unofficially once advised, and it was done unofficially I think because that was practice of Special Branch, they didn't want to say anything that was in any way attributable so that if anybody went public about something then the force could say no such thing was ever said. So these things were done off the record. But I was once advised by the Special Branch people, unofficially, that South Armagh republicans were starting on the groundwork of what could be an attack. Then the ceasefires came. I never got any specific warning in those terms about loyalists, although I'm quite sure that there are some elements within distant loyalism that given half a chance would have thought along those lines."

But when people came to picket the house, they never felt, as a family, "For God's sake, let's get out of here, there's got to be a quieter way to live our lives?" "No." It never crossed his mind? "Oh, you can't say it didn't cross our minds. But insofar as we all toyed with the idea of being somewhere else, it wasn't the push factor in Northern Ireland that was in our minds, it was the pull factor of opportunities that might be elsewhere, which we didn't take up."

Such as? "Oh, there would have been a time when, had I been available in mainland politics, there would have been significant opportunities."

Really? Is he thinking of the time the then *Daily Telegraph* editor Charles Moore mentioned him as a possible leader of the Conservative Party to replace Iain Duncan Smith? Did Trimble regard that as a serious possibility? Declining to disavow the idea, he replies: "Plenty of people in England did." And did he contemplate it? "Ah, not seriously, not beyond the point of saying to ourselves, 'Wouldn't it be nice if we could do that?' But it was not something that we could do."

AFTER PLAYING HIS OWN "Nixon goes to China" role in building the process, part of David Trimble obviously hopes that Sinn Féin and the DUP will prove able to restore it and then consolidate it. But he presumably allows for the possibility that this particular attempt to settle the problem has failed, or is in the process of failing. If it fails, what would he consider the key reasons for its failure?

"The key reasons for the problem that the process has been in over the course of the last number of years has been the failure to resolve the paramilitary issue.

The whole process was predicated on the assumption that the paramilitary organisations were prepared to abandon terrorism and engage wholeheartedly and unambiguously in politics. And that hasn't yet happened in terms. There's clearly been a trend in that direction but it hasn't happened in terms. The fact that there's been some continuing violence, the fact that there has been a failure to decommission and all the things around that has been the root cause of the problem. Had there been unequivocal movement by paramilitaries, then the 28 per cent who voted against in the 1998 referendum would have diminished rather than grown. Most of that 28 per cent wasn't hostility, it was just deep scepticism — and that would have diminished. And if that had diminished then inevitably the DUP would have come into the process willy-nilly. They did come into the process, in fact one of the remarkable things post-1998 is the extent to which right from the outset the DUP came into the process, determined to share the fruits of the process even while still maintaining a formal position of opposition to it. That itself was hugely significant, the huge contrast between 1973 and 1999, so far as the DUP was concerned. That was clear right from the outset."

But what, if anything, did he get wrong? "Well, some people will say that we should not have jumped at the end of November 1999, that we should have toughed that out longer and that I think is probably the point at which you would have a significant number of people in the party saying, 'No, we should have toughed that out.' And then of course the other big point is when you come to the autumn of 2003 — was it wise to engage with republicans on a sequence there? That is one point where I have to say that, given the opportunity, I would have done things differently."

Meaning, he could have fought the election on an entirely different basis? "Well, we were left with no clear basis to fight the election as it turned out, and that and the time of the year contributed to the debacle — debacle's the wrong word, our discomfort, because it wasn't a complete debacle."

Was that not a case in point of him being too accommodating to the British Prime Minister? He had won two victories, forced Blair to cancel the election once, and then a second time. Yet it had seemed to me, watching him and talking to him at the time, that he was almost embarrassed by his success and by the sense that they couldn't keep postponing the election. Yet he surely felt the reason for postponement was as valid in October as it had been in April and May. Why didn't he just go to Blair and say, "We still don't have the basis for forming a government, let's postpone a third time and hang tough until the republicans actually deliver?"

"Well, you're saying I was accommodating to Blair. Unfortunately, that is not in fact the point. Unfortunately the truth is worse, it's more a case of hubris, that we saw Blair and Ahern fail in March and we were

tempted into thinking maybe we could do it better ourselves. And I can't say that we did much better. So it
was more a case of hubris in that sense. Also, in my own
mind there was the question: 'If you delay' — because
we would then be delaying for six months minimum —
'is that actually going to help?' You would then be going
through a winter at the mercy of events, that was in my
mind as much as anything else. In addition, every other
party was calling for elections, some of them quite
hypocritically, and blaming us for the postponement.
We were embarrassed by the image of running away
from the people."

So there was an element almost of fatalism on his
part by that stage? "No, what's in my mind is that rather
than just simply sit back on the oars, and be then at the
mercy of whatever currents occur, it is better to actually
try and take control of the situation and produce something. Where the error was, was the hope, belief that we
could do better, quicker, than Blair and Ahern and in
fact we didn't really do that much better."

Wasn't the strategic miscalculation also this: that
while he was developing confidence in the republicans
— and there's no doubt that there was a change in the
atmospherics between himself and Gerry Adams — no
matter even what Adams might have wanted to do, he'd
watched Trimble battle for survival within unionism for
six years, saw the DUP waiting in the wings and knew
there was absolutely no certainty the UUP could win the

election? In other words, wasn't it blindingly obvious that the IRA was going to hold back until it saw which choice the unionist electorate made and which party republicans would have to deal with after the election?

"Your question reminded me that the other factor that was there progressively during that year was that the position within the party got more and more untenable. Up until that last year, while there were divisions within the party, they were still divisions *within* the party and there was still some sense of the party and some prospect that the party at some point in the future might heal those divisions. But as 2003 unfolded, that became more and more illusory, the position within the party was really deteriorating badly. That was another factor for moving forward rather than back, so that's an element in it too.

"You're right about the change in the atmosphere and that I'd tie to the summer and the determination with which republicans came forward saying, 'Let's try and manage the summer.' And their success in doing that was not achieved easily. They did work very hard to do it, and indeed if you look at the summer of 2004 you can see the same pattern repeated, and repeated actually in more difficult circumstances. They did it, and again at some political and personal cost to some republicans. So that argument about republicans holding back, I'm not sure. There was a holding back, but I'm not sure it was for the political calculation you mention. My own hunch

— I can't prove any of this and this is purely a hypothesis — is that the political leadership within the republican movement were in fact actually committed to doing things in terms that would have satisfied our needs — particularly on the transparency of decommissioning — but the problem came elsewhere in the field and particularly in fields not far from South Armagh, from people in the paramilitary side who didn't want to go ahead with the decommissioning with the implication that it's going to be completed and we're going to wind up the IRA. I think they weren't then, at that stage, prepared for that. And I don't think that that reluctance was due to political factors but due to a factor which we have not yet got the resolution to — which is in what circumstances are people who are making a huge living out of racketeering going to get rid of the muscle that underpins the racketeering as much as anything else. That I think is the problem which has not yet been resolved."

Republicans and others would contend that many weaknesses and difficulties in the process actually derived from Trimble's failure to manage his own party. Did he make a great mistake back in 1998 when he refused to allow the man who would become his chief tormentor — the Lagan Valley MP Jeffrey Donaldson, who had split with him over the issue of IRA decommissioning — to stand for election to the first Assembly? And has it ever occurred to him that the history of the entire period might have been different had he managed to keep Donaldson inside the tent?

"Yes, there are quite a few people in the party who take that view, and indeed that's implicit in the decision that was taken after 2001 to let everyone who wished stand the second time around. It's quite possible you could say that the decision to exclude him in 1998 was wrong, just as the decision to include him in 2003 was wrong. Again this is hindsight, nobody can say for certain. But there have been a significant number of people in the party, and I felt sympathy towards this viewpoint myself, who in retrospect felt we would have been better allowing him in even though that would have meant a more difficult time, at least initially. What always strikes people outside the party as strange is the discovery that the leadership isn't in control. The leadership has never been in control of the party. The party's structures are such that the power does not rest with the leadership, or even the leadership group, but is diffuse throughout the party and so you've difficulty in getting the coherence and discipline that other people expect there to be in the party. And for people outside the party to say, 'well, change the party', well that would have required a two-thirds majority of the Council. Change was not an option and indeed has been quite difficult to achieve."

He says that and I've heard him say it before and I'm still not sure I accept it as the whole picture. Trimble certainly appeared initially in a powerful and driving position. In April 1998 he won an extraordinary margin of victory at the Unionist Council, which backed the Agreement by some 70 to 30 per cent. Even though he was holed close to the water line in the subsequent Assembly election, nationalists and republicans looked at his comfort zone then inside the UUC and concluded Trimble was over-estimating the strength of his internal opponents to gain advantage over Sinn Féin and in his dealings with the government. Then of course his power to drive and enforce policy was actually diminished as his majority fell in the subsequent years, and he found himself holding on by margins of around 52 and 53 per cent. That in turn opened him to the internal unionist charge that he was governing his own party without sufficient consensus among unionists in support of a power-sharing arrangement which depended on the consent of the majority of both communities for its legitimacy. Looking back now — and whatever about the risks he might have taken back in 1998 and 1999 — can he see that he perhaps took unacceptable risks further down the line as his internal majority fell?

"Well I didn't start on that basis, I think you've got to start with the 70/30 split, which is where we were in '98. That's when the policy started. OK, that dropped to 58/42 at the UUC meeting in November 1999. But again, I can't turn round after getting a majority of 57 per cent and say 'I'm not going to go ahead.' By the time you get down to the couple of occasions when there was only a couple of percentage points in it, that question you ask is no longer available to be asked. And even if one's going to suddenly reverse policy, those figures counsel a cautious approach. Those figures are figures that say, 'Try and bring as many people along with you.' That's why in the early days lines were put out to the other wing of the party, that's why Donaldson was included in the talks team on a number of occasions subsequently. And that's why at a number of Council meetings we actually tried to get compromise positions. So the narrow margins were taken account of in terms of party management. But of course the people who complain about party management are complaining about the fact that I did that. The people who said, 'He didn't manage the party' were really saying, 'Oh, he should have just sort of thrown them out, knee-capped them' or whatever, you know, 'enforce discipline by our traditional methods with a baseball bat' or whatever."

Trimble laughs when I count myself firmly out of this category of critics because I had previously suggested in print that his biggest error of judgement in the management of his party came when he snapped after Donaldson and two other MPs resigned the party whip. At a moment when Donaldson plainly acted out of weakness rather than strength — having previously signalled he would 'consider his position', and thus inviting speculation that he was preparing to jump ship and join the DUP — Trimble allowed Donaldson to provoke him and actually moved unsuccessfully to expel him. With the benefit of hindsight would he not concede that that was a huge mistake, given his reduced circumstances and that he was about to take his party into an election? He has already intimated that perhaps he should not have re-engaged with republicans in September/October 2003 and that he had been wrong to think he could bring them "up to the mark" where Blair and Ahern had failed earlier the same year. Does he now accept that, in escalating his internal war — albeit under sustained provocation — he failed to put his party first and thus set the stage for his defeat in the November election and the subsequent defection of Donaldson, ironically the UUP's biggest vote-winner in the Assembly poll?

Trimble's demeanour as much as his words tells that he was already past the point of no return. "The position within the party in 2003 steadily deteriorated and those disciplinary proceedings were a consequence of the deterioration, not a cause. And I think that we were in that territory even before then. Indeed, actually the surprise was by the summer of 2003 that Donaldson hadn't resigned because had he been consistent with what he was doing and saying, he would have done. Then when you had the alternative party launch — the statement about resigning the party whip was like the launch of the alternative party — and consequently there was no alternative left to at that stage. But we were getting towards the end of the road by that point."

It is generally accepted that Donaldson gave the cutting edge to Trimble's internal opposition over those years. That traditional party right, the original 30 percent of "No's", would not have been able to give him the same degree of trouble had Donaldson not been on their side. And I wonder now how Trimble rates him as a politician? He resists this, protesting mildly: "It's not really a fair question because I don't think I'm in a position to give an objective answer to that."

Yet at one time Trimble would clearly have considered Donaldson his likely successor? He doesn't deny that: "Yes, obviously when I took him to Chequers a couple of weeks before the final round of the negotiations to spend all Sunday working through with the Prime Minister and John Holmes the detail of where we were, where we were going and how we were doing it. Obviously when I took him there, leaving Empey and Taylor to one side, that carries with it a very clear indication. And there were times when he would have appeared to be my chief lieutenant. So the fact that he broke from us at the last minute, although it was not clear to me that that was happening . . ."

On that Good Friday afternoon? "Yes, it was not clear to me that that was happening. Even after we'd taken the decision to endorse it, after the party officers decided, not unanimously but collectively. I then cross the corridor to where everybody else was in the big party room, told them this was our decision, this is what we were going to do. There wasn't any murmur, you know, people accepted that, and it was at that point I turned round and I said, 'Right, I'm going up, who's coming up with me?' I knew there was a limited number of places there and I thought there'd be competition for them. Rather than me choose, people were left to sort it out amongst themselves. And while a number of people were mentioning Jeffrey, he quietly said, 'Do you mind David if I'm left out at this stage?' He'd expressed opposition but not to the point of indicating that he's going to walk out or resign or whatever. He said, 'Do you mind if I sit this one out?' or something along those lines. And the terms that he used, the tone that he used, gave me no hint. Indeed, I was quite taken by surprise later when I was doing the press conference and Eamon Mallie asked me to comment on Donaldson's walkout. I was surprised by that and of course in the immediate aftermath one's intention was, 'Can we sort this out, can we get people back together again?' Beyond that I really don't want to comment on the purely personal aspects of this, it's too close, it's too recent."

I am just about to acquiesce in this and move on when Trimble adds tantalisingly: "Except . . . but you won't want to print it. . . . Actually, no, I can't say it because you will want to print it. . . ." Well, obviously I do now. Go on, I urge him. "Ach," comes the less than flattering assessment of Donaldson's political skills, "He could have beaten me if he'd tried. He always drew

back, he always lost his nerve. With a little bit more —
I'm not quite sure what the 'something' was — but certainly in those meetings when we had negotiations on
compromise motions he always folded."

So Trimble went in to more than one of those meetings thinking Donaldson had the advantage? "Look, my
chaps before each Council meeting did a careful canvass,
and their collective wisdom was given to me before each
meeting, in a figure. And the actual outcome of the vote
was never more than one per cent away from the figure
that was given. On the famous occasion in 2002 they told
me, 'You're going to lose.'"

It had often occurred to me that Donaldson missed
his moment in fact when the Rev Martin Smyth
mounted a surprisingly strong leadership challenge at
two days' notice before the UUC Annual Meeting on 25
March 2000 and claimed 43.2 per cent of the vote. I
thought then that had Donaldson joined the fray the
whole thing would have unravelled, Trimble would
have had less than 50 per cent on the first ballot, and
thereafter his support would have melted away. Water
under the bridge now, of course. But Trimble does not
disagree: "That's not impossible."

Chapter Nine

Which Majority?

IN ONE VITAL RESPECT DAVID TRIMBLE lost his majority long before the November 2003 elections. Two years before, in October 2001, having resigned again the previous July to force the issue of IRA decommissioning, he sought re-election as First Minister and was denied the requisite majority of designated unionist votes by the defection of two party colleagues. Four days later, in a manoeuvre he had said in advance would be "tacky", Trimble secured a return to office courtesy of three Alliance Party members and one member of the Women's Coalition re-designating themselves as "unionist" for that purpose. Wasn't it tacky? Worse than that, didn't it send a dangerous and damaging signal to unionists that the rules, including those requiring cross-community consent, could be broken on a whim? And would not the honourable thing then have been to resign and allow the election that should have followed under the rules to take place?

I know Trimble has never cared for this argument. "No," he returns defiantly, "I never saw the issue in the terms that you did. We were in difficulty because a couple of members of my party who were elected on a pro-Agreement manifesto had ratted on it. The dishonourable conduct was theirs, and that meant that we had to get involved in what I concede was an undignified situation. But I did not regard myself as having lost my mandate within unionism because that stemmed from votes cast by the people rather than the conduct of two assembly members."

But unionists always argued that need for consent implied the right to say "no", and in a democracy people have the right to change their mind. Now Trimble had been rejected for re-election as First Minister by a majority of unionist assembly members. And way beyond the internal politics of his unionist party, I press him for this reason: the principle of dual consent by a majority of both communities had been enshrined in the Agreement. By opening the door to that scenario, by allowing re-designation in order to overcome what by then was a majority against him, wasn't he also opening the door to a situation in which a minority of unionists could one day prove acceptable as part of a simple pro-Agreement majority to keep the Agreement afloat in defiance even of the wishes of a unionist majority?

"I'll repeat what I said about the lack of legitimacy in that vote. That was my clear starting point in it, that if people had stood by their election manifesto, they would have been voting for me and I've not much time for other arguments on the issue. And no, I don't see the other point in the terms that you express it anyway. These arrangements which are there, particularly these safeguard arrangements, I have never regarded as immutable. I can give you any number of arguments as to why these complex arrangements are a bad idea in theory, and they are. I mean all, all these arrangements which are designed to move away from a straight democratic process to one where you've got these special mechanisms. The special mechanisms were necessary in order to get an Agreement because of the lack of confidence that existed within the political system in Northern Ireland as a whole for a pure, simple democratic process, which of course is a majoritarian process. Because of the lack of confidence for that, we had to have all these checks and balances but that produces a slightly artificial situation which is not good in the long run because in the long run you'll be in a position where there is no opposition and consequently the electorate are deprived of the opportunity of choosing between political policies that might be offered to them. That's the whole purpose of an election. Now the electorate clearly were endorsing what we were doing in the Agreement in setting up an assembly, operating on these special procedures. But in the long run that would not be a good thing, and in the long run that would not be acceptable to the electorate. So there will be a period in time, ten years' time, twenty years' time, whatever, where these special features will disappear. Of that I'm quite convinced."

A couple of years back, Sinn Féin's Mitchel McLaughlin was surveying Trimble's struggle for survival within the UUP and suggested it might be necessary to lower the cross-community threshold in order to allow a simple pro-Agreement majority to prevail. McLaughlin made no secret of the fact that he contemplated this change in order to cope with what seemed even then the likely emergence of an anti-Agreement majority on the unionist side. And as a republican he plainly would have no difficulty with the concept of a minority unionist party providing the cross-community cover for an executive then largely composed of nationalists. But Trimble is effectively saying over time he can envisage precisely that situation? "Yeah, yeah," he readily agrees.

This strikes me — as did the Alliance re-designation trick at the time — as a quite extraordinary position for a unionist leader. The Belfast Agreement was regarded rightly as a victory for John Hume's persistent argument that majoritarianism does not work in a divided society. Famously described by Seamus Mallon as "Sunningdale for Slow Learners", by which he meant Sinn Féin, it also brought even the most recalcitrant unionist face-to-face with the reality that unionism could not expect to govern Northern Ireland on any sort of Westminster model courtesy of its simple majority. This was compulsory coalition rather than the voluntary arrangement Craig and Trimble had failed to sell to unionists back in the seventies. Indeed, it went beyond the concept of proportionality, and when the first executive was formed it failed to reflect even the fact of an overall unionist majority in the Assembly.

Few in the outside world would suggest that unionists deserve any brownie points for this painfully slow response to the changed realities in Northern Ireland and the claims of justice and even-handedness. And Hume was manifestly right: majoritarianism would not work in that divided society. Even the ascendant Democratic Unionists have bowed to that fact. But what Trimble is now saying, if I understand him correctly, is that — while Hume's triumph has removed any form of unionist majoritarianism — a different form of majoritarianism could assume legitimacy and within which unionism would be a minority?

"No. No. I'm not saying that. And indeed in your overview there is an over-statement of the position in regard to this. One of the things that people forget about the Northern Ireland Executive and Assembly is that the principal way of proceeding to take a decision is by majority vote and that the number of occasions in the lifetime of the Assembly when there was anything other than a majority vote were a handful."

Yes, but on key issues like the election of the co-equal First and Deputy First Ministers the higher threshold did apply? "Yes, there were certain particular issues where you had to have the special majority, but 90 per cent of the votes were on a majoritarian basis. What I'm saying is that I think those special provisions, those special occasions, where you have to have something other than a majority will, in the not too distant future, disappear."

I understand that that is indeed what Trimble is saying. But the consequence of that surely is that you can end up in a situation where there is a pro-Agreement majority — comprising largely nationalists and republicans, plus the Alliance Party and a minority unionist rump — who could form a government and simply bypass the fact that there is an anti-Agreement majority within unionism?

"If there is a move at some point in the future towards simple democratic majoritarianism, then of course that majority could be constructed in a whole lot of different ways," Trimble confirms.

And that must mean it is capable of being constructed in a way that permanently excludes a majority of unionism? Trimble is insistent: "No. You're saying permanently, that's quite wrong."

But is it? If the majority of unionists came to the view that they didn't want the executive at all, or didn't wish to appoint First and Deputy First Ministers, a minority of unionists in that scenario plus Sinn Féin, plus SDLP and Alliance could simply over-rule them? Trimble argues: "But that wouldn't be permanent."

Well, it would at least be for the lifetime of an Assembly. "Well, it might be, it might not. If one moves to
the position where we operate in the future by simple
majoritarianism, then you're right back at the start. You
made a starting point of an evolution within unionism.
If a majority of the people elected are unionists, then I
think unionism as a whole cannot regard itself as being
in a minority position, even if at any one particular time
the administration is formed with only a minority of unionists in it. That's a consequence of the electoral process
and what people decide to do. And I can also tell you
that one of the options we are looking at as a party — in
the event of there being an agreement between DUP and
Sinn Féin — is that we won't take office, and we'll become the opposition."

INFORMING A LOT OF THESE QUESTIONS is the charge by
some of Trimble's most severe critics (and indeed it
might truthfully be said by some who generally support
him) that the decisions and judgements he has made,
and the risks he has run — personally, and more particularly with his party — have been driven above all by
his desire to be First Minister of Northern Ireland and to
cling to that office. He would obviously reject that. But
looking back, would he accept that in the re-designation
business he appeared at least to play fast-and-loose with

the entitlements of the unionist people? And can he allow that perhaps he asked and expected his party to pay
too high a price for his devotion to this project?

There is a long sigh before he replies: "No, I can't.
We were supported at every stage by a majority of the
party which, while it appeared a bare majority of UUC
delegates at times, was a very substantial majority of
activists and an even greater majority of UUP voters. I
think the people who kept the party divided have a lot
to answer for in terms of this. It was always remarkable
to us that those people who in an earlier age were the
greatest advocates of majority rule were the last people
ever to accept majority decisions. And I think there is a
lot in that, and that a lot of the responsibility for the decline in the party's position lies with those who would
not accept majority decisions. That is the first point I
would make on that.

"In terms of the earlier part of your question, I was
not keen on being First Minister and I never enjoyed being First Minister. You'll find that reflected by a number
of the people who were there. Yes, I was attracted to dealing with the politics of the situation, bored to death by the
administration. The one point where my interest in the
administration picked up was when we started through
the Re-investment Reform Initiative to develop some real
policies of our own and we started to actually make a
change. Up until then we were really just continuing the
existing policy format of the direct rule administration.

Some people got quite excited about being involved in the minutiae of this, and writing letters about it, meetings, interest groups and all the rest. I did not find that particularly interesting. The high politics of it, yes. I was interested in that and I was anxious to succeed in what you might call the project that we'd undertaken."

The high politics, for sure. But what about the high profile and high theatre, the banquets at Buckingham Palace, the visits to the White House and so on? Might First Minister Trimble have enjoyed this aspect of things a little too much?

With no hint of irony, he says: "I don't know what 'too much' is on this. There were occasions, I must confess, aspects of that I enjoyed. It would be quite wrong to say otherwise. But a number of those aspects, particularly when you're talking about the state banquets and all the rest of it, those came through leadership of the party and I would have had them anyway as leader of the party. I would have had those things, as my predecessor did, so no. As I say, I was attracted by the high politics of the situation, I was attracted to the possibility of actually achieving something and that was the main driver there."

IF THE DUP AND SINN FÉIN manage to make an agreement and to carry it through, I can see that a lot of Trimble's colleagues might feel hurt because, as Sir Reg Empey once remarked, the DUP had left the Ulster

Unionists to do "the heavy lifting". On the other hand, Trimble could claim vindication in that, just as Hume had created the architecture for the settlement, Trimble would be seen as the man who moved unionism to a place it had to go in order to secure the Union and lay the basis for a stable Northern Ireland. And in that event, while it might be of concern to unionist politicians wanting a political career, the outside world will not remotely care what the balance is between Ulster Unionists and Democratic Unionists, provided the power-sharing settlement survives. If, on the other hand, there is no durable agreement, if the DUP and Sinn Féin cannot bridge the gap, then Trimble's sacrifice of his party as the dominant force within unionism will have been for nothing. Does he accept that?

"No I don't accept that. May I just comment on the first scenario — that if there is an agreement between Sinn Féin and the DUP in the course of the next year or two — yes, you can say this may be what secures the process and that the rest of the world won't care much about the balance of unionist forces. But in the long run, the Democratic Unionist Party cannot be the major vehicle for the unionist electorate. I mentioned earlier about the increasing disenchantment about politics from the 'garden centre Prod' whose disenchantment is partly because politics can't achieve things but more because he dislikes the style, the character and particularly the sectarian manner of local politics. And the very strong sectarian element that exists within the DUP and is reflected in DUP politics is one that runs against the grain of unionism today. By unionism, I mean the people who identify themselves as a unionist, who are actual or potential unionist voters. So in the long run, they are not going to be able to be the vehicle for unionist opinion as a whole unless their U-turns over the Agreement are then matched by even greater U-turns over their sectarianism."

I can understand that argument in the context of the internal unionist debate over the past 30 years. However, won't it lose its relevance to a considerable degree in a post-Paisley era?

"The Free Presbyterian character of the DUP does not depend purely on Dr Paisley. It's in the DNA of that party." So he does not accept that Peter Robinson or Nigel Dodds could assume the leadership and gradually re-invent the DUP? "No, they're not going to be able to adjust themselves to the increasingly secular character of politics. They will not be able to. I think where we are at in terms of the DUP having just got their nose in front of us in terms of the popular vote is I think temporary. 'Temporary' may on this occasion be a number of years; I'm not assuming that things are just going to automatically quickly flow back our way. And indeed, if the DUP provide the final coping stone to the efforts that we've made to secure the Agreement, then there will be I imagine a short-term electoral benefit for them in so doing.

I'm just making a point that, in view of the DNA of the party, they cannot in the long run provide the vehicle for moderate majority unionists."

Trimble entered into all of this to win back lost ground for unionism, with a determination above all to make sure unionism didn't again fall for "the blame game". The hope in the Northern Ireland Office and presumably in Number 10 as well is that the triumph of Sinn Féin and the DUP presents opportunity because neither party can be out-flanked. That's a reasonable hope and yet, presumably, there are also dangers here. How does Trimble see those dangers, particularly in light of what he has said about the DUP and its character?

"I think the danger is that they may lack the capacity to deal with the situation that they're in. We've been talking about what the position would be if they do manage to do a deal with republicans that revives the Agreement, and the Assembly and all the rest of it. I think the greater danger is in terms of their failure. There is an element of republicans that wanted to marginalise unionism. There's a general attitude within nationalism about wanting to portray nice nationalists and nasty Prods. Now, we won 'the blame game' right up until the suspension in October 2002. But sooner or later, the republicans are going to try to bounce the blame back, and sooner or later they will come forward with an offer, and if the DUP turn that down unreasonably, then we'll be in a different context. And then there will be a danger of unionism beginning to drift towards the margins again."

And he means that that danger is greater because the DUP as the lead unionist party is easier to blame or more easily characterised across the world as an intransigent, unreasonable party because of its sectarian character?

"Yes," he affirms. And does Dr Paisley in his view have it within him to turn his back on a lifetime of oppositionist politics and make the historic rapprochement? Again: "You're putting too much emphasis on Dr Paisley. He's not alone. A large chunk of the party will share his views. Within the party activists, there is significant support for his view. And there are senior party people too for whom this is a black-and-white issue, this is a struggle between good and evil. With good being the DUP and what it represents and evil being republicanism and what that represents. And for those people, I cannot see how they can reconcile themselves to any form of arrangement whereby the Assembly functions again with a government in which the leading positions are shared by DUP and Sinn Féin. I can't see how that segment of the party will ever move in that direction. As to individuals, who knows?"

Does he at least accept that people like Peter Robinson and Nigel Dodds are people of sufficient political grasp and realism, with the necessary street craft and all the rest of it . . . that they know where the future lies and the accommodations that have to be made?

"I'll deal with the party rather than individuals. The DUP has been here before. They were here before in 1975, when Dr Paisley and the Rev William Beattie joined with others in asking Sir Robert Lowry to draw up proposals for a voluntary coalition. They told him that this was what they wanted to see. However they might re-interpret their participation in that meeting, the DUP were there in the Atkins Talks, particularly when the second White Paper proposed two models, one of which was crafted to meet the DUP ideas and to provide them with a way in which they could create an assembly in which power would be shared without them having to agree it. And they didn't come up to the mark on that. Now if they finally do what they failed to do in 1975 and 1982, we shall see. But the historic record points more towards failure than success."

Chapter Ten

Conclusion

D ID HE DESERVE HIS NOBEL PEACE PRIZE? Readers coming fresh to this subject might think that to pose this question is something of an affront. Yet David Trimble's Nobel award was attended by considerable degrees of doubt, and no end of sheer begrudgery, particularly from some nationalists.

There was always going to be an element of Trimble as the "prophet not without honour", save in his own country. Until he was confirmed joint winner with John Hume in 1999, unionists hadn't exactly been in the business of collecting peace prizes. To the contrary: through their bitter experience of the IRA's long "war", much of the unionist community would come to associate "peace campaigners" — and what is today disparagingly described in some political circles as "the human rights industry" — with nationalist and republican propaganda. Unionists didn't "do" peace and human rights.

Placed in context, this was not so daft or inexplicable as it would appear today. It wasn't that unionists had no interest in peace or in human rights. Rather they saw themselves at the receiving end of a ruthlessly efficient IRA campaign which trampled their rights underfoot — including in so many instances the basic right to life — while much of the outside world appeared either unsympathetic or, worse, to actually understand what might be called "the causes of terrorism". And it is interesting to note that modern unionist leaders — like Trimble, and also the next generation of DUP leaders like Peter Robinson, Nigel Dodds, Gregory Campbell and Jeffrey Donaldson — can at times show rather greater enthusiasm for certain of the provisions of the European Convention than some senior politicians in London and Dublin.

It is also true that some central unionist politicians will today acknowledge, at least in private, that the hardline heave which toppled the moderate Northern Ireland Prime Minister of the day, Terence O'Neill, was a profound mistake and that unionism's general response to the demands of the civil rights movement was deeply and damagingly ill-judged. Some of course would also contend that the errors of successive United Kingdom governments in London deserved equal criticism.

Hindsight, however, is a marvellous thing. Back then, even "modernisers" like Brian Faulkner sent unionists conflicting and misleading signals — appearing to reject some of the arguments of civil rights campaigners on principle, but then bowing to the pressure for reform out of perceived political weakness.

Such weakness left the moderates easy prey to the increasingly dominant Vanguard leader William Craig and Ian Paisley who reinforced unionist fears that the civil rights campaign was but a front for a fresh republican assault on the state itself. And then, of course, the birth of the Provisional IRA and the emergence of a new generation of republicans determined to drive the Brits out of Ireland and to coerce unionist Ulster into a united Ireland, rendered this assessment self-fulfilling, if for some also self-serving.

Having lost the propaganda battle at the outset, and finding themselves invariably cast as "the guilty party", unionists looked into the long night of "the Troubles" in a mood of deepening bitterness, alienation, insecurity and fear. Hence this inclination to interpret talk of "human rights" as code for complaint about anti-Catholic discrimination, and suggested "peace initiatives" as code for what they always feared — a deal between the British government and their IRA tormentors. Indeed, some unionists remained in a defensive, if not apologetic, mode for most of the subsequent 27 years of direct rule when British ministers exercised exclusive responsibility for the governance of Northern Ireland.

It was only gradually in the late 1980s that some unionist politicians began to draw the succour and encouragement they could from the SDLP's consistent stand against IRA violence, and John Hume's repeated asser-

tion that there was no state of injustice to justify the taking of a single life in Northern Ireland.

Yet there was also deep and enduring distrust of
Hume. Unionists generally believed that for him it must
be "a united Ireland or nothing" and would invariably
interpret his talk after Bloody Sunday 1972 of "an agreed
Ireland" as code for unity by other means. They saw evidence for this in the exclusion of unionism from the processes which led to the Anglo-Irish Agreement in 1985.
And they were hopelessly indisposed to revise their
thinking even after a seminal interview with this writer in
The Irish Times in January 1990 in which Hume set out the
framework for what would become the Belfast Agreement eight long years later; dual referendums in which
the people in the North and the people in the south
would effectively copper-fasten Northern Ireland's constitutional position and finally lay the basis for nationalist
consent for the arrangements for the policing of the state.

Had the unionist leadership of the day engaged with
Hume's agenda at that point they might have been better equipped to deal with the political challenges thrown
at them by the subsequent Hume/Adams dialogue. Instead, and perversely, unionism's failure to engage with
him would inform its subsequent fear that, in opening
his dialogue with the Sinn Féin president, Hume had
abandoned any thought of dealing with unionists and
had by then "much bigger fish to fry."

Hence the collective raspberry from what Sinn Féin would term "rejectionist unionists" when Trimble was named joint Nobel winner with Hume. For as he reminds us here, the belief was widespread in the unionist community that a secret deal between the Provisionals and the British could be the only explanation for the second IRA ceasefire in 1997. And in the eyes of the so-called rejectionists (who were roughly half the unionist electorate, let it be remembered, even in 1998), Trimble was Judas, his Nobel prize money the equivalent of thirty pieces of silver.

Even some moderate unionists who supported the Belfast Agreement would be a touch embarrassed by Trimble's award. It was possible for them to convince themselves that Trimble had outflanked the republicans or that the British had tricked them into a partitionist settlement. But did they really want their leader lumbered with an award for actually making peace with republicans? And what would the unionist electorate make of it?

Beyond unionism too there was doubt as to whether Trimble really was the right man to accompany Hume to the award ceremony in Oslo in December 1999.

For nationalists, and indeed for some ultra-moderate unionists, the question was obvious. What about Gerry Adams? Had not he done as much for peace, if not more, than David Trimble by persuading the Provisional IRA and its Sinn Féin allies to abandon the "armalite and ballot box" strategy? Should it not have been Hume/

Adams who were rewarded in recognition of their politically and personally dangerous adventure? Or at the
very least Hume, Adams and Trimble?

Now, as then, it was also possible to divine in some
quarters an underlying assessment that "peace" was
something that almost had to be forced upon the unionists and loyalists. For even among some nationalist politicians, intellectually clear about the need for an accommodation, there was an almost irresistible instinct to regard the "hopeless" and "friendless" unionists as the
sad Irish equivalent of the extreme white South Afri-
kaner in need of a de Klerk figure to help them face the
reality of their position.

The suspicion among his friends is that some of the
real and abiding nationalist irritation with David Trimble was that he would prove them wrong, turn the tables
and present an acceptable face of unionism to the outside world. What was worse from this unforgiving perspective was that the early Trimble had shown so much
promise in terms of living-up to the unionist stereotype.

Hence this book begins with the perception of David
Trimble as the angry man of unionism. But, as he records here with some satisfaction, the angry man of
Garvaghy Road fame was to disappoint many nationalists or republicans who may have been hoping for a
"tribal" victory over recalcitrant unionism.

Recalcitrance, I think, was never really David Trimble's problem, although many — including some who

would wish to be persuaded otherwise — remain un-
convinced. During many conversations over the years, I
have listened to Sinn Féin chairman Mitchel McLaughlin
bemoan Trimble's failure to "face-down" the rejectionist
wing of the Ulster Unionist Party. And he is far from
alone in suspecting to this day that Trimble used the internal opposition for so long led by Jeffrey Donaldson in
order to evade his responsibilities under the Belfast
Agreement. Yet in the same time I have observed and
reported what I believe was a genuine change in Gerry
Adams's assessment and his realisation that, while republicans on the ground considered Trimble "a messer"
and "a waster", he was, as he would put it to me, "the
best messer we've got".

In this book I ask Trimble about his historic handshake with Adams. One of my script readers suggested I
omit the question about the moment, the sense of the
occasion, and whether it brought a lump to the throat or
a tear to the eye. On reflection, however, I have left it in
because these two men, at that moment, were making
huge personal as well as political history.

And having spent much of the summer of 2004 in
conversation with David Trimble, it seems clear to me by
any criteria that he did indeed deserve his Nobel Prize.

It is entirely arguable that Adams deserved to share
it with Trimble and Hume. And I offer no contrary
judgement about that here. However, I am pretty certain

too, from my long conversations with him, that Gerry Adams would not deny Trimble's entitlement.

Here was a leader of a unionism laid low by a combination of history and past experience, the constraints imposed by its own sectarian inheritance and instinctive siege mentality, the self-delusions and inadequacies of its leaderships, its capacity for political growth stunted by a punishing terrorist campaign and faced with varying degrees of hostility and indifference on the part of successive British governments, when — after 25 years of warfare — the IRA suddenly invited London to sue for peace. The Hume/Adams dialogue meanwhile had resulted in a "pan-nationalist" consensus stretching all the way from Taoiseach Albert Reynolds's office in Leinster House to the Oval Office in the Clinton White House.

Not for nothing did Trimble's predecessor Jim Molyneaux fear what he thought at the time might result in the greatest threat to unionism since the partition of Ireland and the establishment of the Northern Ireland state. Reynolds caught the prevailing mood of mockery at the time, asking, "Who can be afraid of peace?"

It was never obviously Molyneaux's view that genuine peace would of itself "de-stabilise" Northern Ireland. The point was that many unionists were afraid because, as Trimble says here, they assumed that the proferred "peace" would prove to be predicated on a secret agenda developed by the British and the republicans during the long years of secret contacts conducted by intermediaries through back-channels the existence of which British ministers had always denied.

Not the least of David Trimble's historic role, from a unionist perspective, would be to engage in the process and keep his nerve long enough to help explode that particular myth.

However, what guarantees his place in history is that he was able to rise above the natural fears and suspicions of his own people — even as he shared them — realising that the offer of a genuine peace was one that should be grasped.

Some commentators have suggested that Molyneaux's response to the first IRA ceasefire was in fact a good deal more sophisticated than is generally allowed; and that, had he been younger and at an earlier stage of his leadership, he might have been more successful in the subsequent negotiations over the Framework Documents. And it is true that Molyneaux and others around him did admit the possibility of eventually dealing with Sinn Féin as a normal political party. However, he and they added the rider that this could only be after a suitable and lengthy period of "quarantine".

This is the crucial contrast with Trimble. As one keen observer puts it: "Molyneaux and those guys were never serious about dealing and the only result of their strategy would have been more violence. This was Trimble's genius. He understood that if the republicans were going to be politicised you had to do it now."

There were of course powerful incentives for Trimble to engage. Even if, in the beginning, it was largely a matter of tactics, no unionist leader could hope to avoid losing "the blame game" if he actually refused to play. And while such unionist leverage as there was — and I think this was always greatly exaggerated — was fast running out during the dying days of the Major government at Westminster, the highly energetic and committed Mo Mowlam had fostered high hopes among nationalists and republicans that an incoming Blair government would be ready to do serious business. As the Progressive Unionist Party's David Ervine was among the first to comprehend, the new Prime Minister would also be augmented by a massive body of Labour backbenchers, many of whom had learned their politics in the 1960s and would likely be instinctively pro-nationalist if not actually anti-unionist.

In theory Trimble might have reverted to the "masterly inactivity" which had served Molyneaux relatively well for most of his leadership of the Ulster Unionist Party. But had he done so, it is clear unionists really would have had cause to fear. For Blair's new broom already promised an era of constitutional reform in Britain, and the still bleak sectarian stalemate that was Northern Ireland would have presented an ugly blot on the changing political landscape of a United Kingdom Blair at one highly ambitious stage thought to re-invent as a "young country". It is also certain that Blair would have found the sectarian stranglehold, and all the justifications it had long provided for doing nothing, personally unacceptable. And beyond all that, the simple bottom line was that no British Prime Minister was going to invite Irish republicans to go back to war because he had no political process to offer them. In that sense at least, Adams was right to assert that the peace process was unstoppable.

The reality therefore was that the mainstream unionist party of the day — first under Molyneaux, then at the critical moment under Trimble, in September 1997 when Sinn Féin was finally admitted to the talks — had no choice but to join the process. Had they refused, the result would have been a liberated Labour government free to embrace fully the pan-nationalist agenda, and thereafter join nationalists and republicans and their supporters around the world in diagnosing rejectionist unionism as the remaining "problem" to be resolved.

Yet as Trimble also makes clear, he did not consider himself in a position of weakness from the outset in his dealings with Tony Blair. His closest political intimates over the years would in fact complain about the "defeatist" mentality of some of his senior party colleagues. And it seems perfectly clear that, having had enough of being considered part of the problem, Trimble decided when the moment came to make unionism part of the solution. From an initial tactical engagement, he would finally come to accept the bona fides of the republican leadership of Gerry Adams and Martin McGuinness. And in the end he enthusiastically joined the two governments in constructing the bridge which would bring Sinn Féin not just in from the cold, but straight to the old Stormont cabinet room and into the devolved government.

Who would have believed it, really? The new terms for the political trade in Northern Ireland are familiar by now. However, "partnership" and "inclusivity" were hardly the unionist fashion even in early 1998, or for that matter back in 1995 when Trimble assumed the leadership. And it is possible, with the passage of time, to forget just how extraordinary was Trimble's decision to go for it, let alone his ability to sell it to his party's ruling council.

It is worth repeating: it was an extraordinarily big thing that David Trimble did, and the more so because he had given his party and his supporters virtually no indication that he would be prepared to travel so far. Indeed, the distance travelled would trigger the biggest convulsions in unionism since 1974.

One respected nationalist insider I spoke to during the preparation of this book repeated his admiration for Trimble's courage, while voicing again the familiar doubt as to whether he ever really attempted to "sell" the Agreement to the unionist people, or at any rate adequately. "I always had the sense that he was part believer, part sceptic," says this source. "And I always wondered if he had been a little bit more of one and less of the other, if he had been prepared to lead the charge right from the beginning, might he have been more successful?"

At times in my coverage of events subsequent to the Good Friday accord I, too, wondered if Trimble actually found himself "conflicted" over the Agreement. He was admittedly holed pretty close to the water mark following the 1998 elections, with an uncomfortably small majority which he would see evaporate during the lifetime of the first Assembly. Even so — and unfamiliar then with this concept of transition by which he explains his thought and decision-making processes now — I found his failure even to move into a shadow administration in 1998 and early 1999 at odds with the Agreement as I understood it. Did delay not in fact strengthen his opponents and rein-force unionist doubts about the whole enterprise?

Likewise, when Trimble first welcomed the publica-tion of the British government's legislation to effect the prisoner release programme, only to vote against it at Second Reading in the House of Commons. Was he in denial? Or (and it would not be the last time I would ask) had he quite simply lost the run of himself? And of course, such suspicions and doubts were magnified for many when Trimble eventually "jumped first" and formed the power-sharing administration without any IRA decommissioning, having maintained that the Ulster Unionists and Sinn Féin would have to "jump together".

One of Trimble's allies of the time once followed me onto a BBC radio programme to complain that I was typical of a particular problem with which the Ulster Unionists were having to contend — namely journalists who had either not read the Belfast Agreement or who had difficulty understanding it. My crime had been to confirm my understanding that IRA decommissioning was not defined in the Agreement as a pre-condition for Sinn Féin's entry into government.

In fairness, the Ulster Unionist belief that it was intended to be a pre-condition had been fortified, not just by Blair's sidebar letter, but also by his famous handwritten pledges delivered during the 1998 referendum campaign. But the Trimble ally was in my view wrong, and any who had harboured any doubt about the matter would finally conclude that the Ulster Unionists had been wrong all along when they performed their dramatic U-turn and entered government with Sinn Féin without having secured IRA decommissioning.

Mo Mowlam for the British government would subsequently endorse the Ulster Unionist view that decommissioning was "an obligation" under the Agreement. And Tony Blair himself flatly rejected hostile unionist suggestions that the Agreement had actually separated Sinn Féin and the IRA and so "sold the pass" on decommissioning altogether. Blair in fact would never depart from his oft-repeated view that the IRA and Sinn Féin were "inextricably linked" and thus continued to expect the Sinn Féin leadership to deliver on the IRA's obligation. In the end, however, it was only the Ulster Unionists, supported by the Conservative Party at Westminster, who would maintain that decommissioning was a pre-condition, and to no effect. The argument was lost.

No matter, as Seamus Mallon would later importantly confirm, Senator Mitchell's clear understanding, expressed at the end of the Review preceding Trimble's decision to form the Executive, that it was based on absolute clarity that decommissioning would have to follow within a period of just six weeks. Nobody would believe that the unionists would have jumped first had they not in fact been obliged to do so under the precise terms of the Agreement. Why would they? The risks for Trimble were massive. He himself suggests here that had Jeffrey Donaldson possessed more of "the killer instinct" he might have finished Trimble off during one of those endless challenges at the Ulster Unionist Council. And why worry about losing the blame game if the Agreement clearly imposed the prior obligation on the republicans?

It is now widely accepted that there was a serious weakness in Trimble's position on IRA decommissioning which would do him and his party much harm. However, it is his evidence here on this issue which persuades me that my nationalist friend is wrong. Trimble was always more believer than sceptic. And while he may have come perilously close to losing the run of himself at times, neither, I believe, was he ever much in denial.

To the contrary, I think his account confirms that David Trimble was really a rather big man grappling with big ideas and some very big and difficult decisions.

For the nature of his real weakness on decommissioning is laid bare. True, he makes a reasonable fist of arguing that "the linkage" between decommissioning, prisoner releases and Sinn Féin's entry into government was always there. The weakness was that he was telling the unionist electorate that that linkage was in the Agreement with a certainty and clarity that did not exist, and could not have existed.

And it is Trimble himself who tells us why; because to have pressed for clarity and certainty on this issue on that famous Good Friday afternoon would have resulted in no agreement and the Ulster Unionists falling for the blame game.

From that afternoon in 1998, when a unionist aide thrust a copy of Tony Blair's famous "sidebar letter" into my hand, I had always had a difficulty with the UUP's line on the decommissioning issue. As previously observed, government lawyers would have had no problem whatsoever drafting an agreement which inextricably linked decommissioning, prisoner releases and Sinn Féin's entry into government, had that been the requirement. But as Trimble starkly admits, this was not a legal document with all the necessary certainty provided by a solicitor handling the sale or purchase of the family home. And while some of us might have attached great weight to the notion of the Agreement as an internationally binding treaty between two sovereign governments, Trimble the constitutional lawyer is altogether more laid back: "And how many treaties are precise, without their opacities and all the rest of it?" he demands.

Precisely so. But it is a bit difficult to claim clarity and certainty for a document you say is elsewhere characterised by opacity. And it was the opacity, arguably, that did for him in the end.

There is no doubt that the reform of policing and the loss of the RUC's "royal" title cost Trimble and his party dear. And even some of his supporters are amazed to this day by Trimble's apparent lack of feel for the internal unionist politics of this issue and for its resonance in the wider unionist community.

Yet I am taken with Trimble's response when I put it to him that, for all his public fury over Patten, he perhaps reckoned this was pain necessary to the process of political change.

In theory, he could have saved the RUC title by seeking to exclude the symbolic issues from the Patten Commission's terms of reference, or by subsequently making it a resignation issue in his dealings with Blair. However, the evidence suggests that on policing, as on decommissioning, Trimble concluded that to demand explicitly unionist terms by definition unacceptable to republicans would have meant no agreement on Good Friday 1998. I am pretty sure he also reckons that had the IRA delivered on decommissioning he and his party would not have lost so significantly from policing reform because the end result would have been the Ulster Unionists co-operating with the SDLP on the Policing Board.

In any event, it is arguable that it was the opacity over decommissioning — which in the end required his party to "jump first", having all along insisted it would not — that marked the beginning of the loss of trust which would contribute to the Democratic Unionist Party's electoral triumph in November 2003.

That certainly will be the judgement of Trimble's unionist detractors. However, it seems to me this is precisely what might prompt sceptical republicans, nationalists and others to revisit their assessment of the man. For it is clear from his own account that it was Trimble the politician, and not Trimble the nit-picking lawyer he would sometimes appear, who negotiated the Agreement. He signed off on it with all its "opacities" because he wanted to gamble on the bona fides of the republican leadership. Not quite believing them, but wanting to, he opted for the transition he hoped would end in a clear and unequivocal republican embrace of exclusively peaceful and democratic politics. And he did so because he too could see the great prize that lay at the end of that road for all the peoples of Northern Ireland and of these islands.

I am struck now by Trimble's candid admission that it was hubris which led him to think he could succeed in that final negotiation with Gerry Adams and Sinn Féin where Tony Blair and Bertie Ahern had failed earlier in 2003. It had certainly seemed clear to me that autumn that it was in fact Trimble's fidelity to the Belfast Agreement which would probably ensure his and his party's defeat in the ensuing Assembly election at the hands of Paisley's DUP.

Again unionist critics, and even some who have supported him, will now feel that he took too many risks with his party. Any leader after all is but a temporary custodian of his party's interests. And in other matters too — his agreement in the end to allow the temporary "re-designation" of non-unionist Assembly members to ensure his re-election as First Minister, and his suggestion that the existing cross-community mechanisms for operating the Assembly and electing an Executive are not immutable — will invite the view in some quarters that he has also been cavalier with protections and guarantees which are more properly the concern of the wider unionist electorate beyond the Ulster Unionist Party.

Having so stretched his party, however, it causes Trimble loyalists furious agonies of pain and grief to hear some nationalists and republicans still question the extent of his commitment to this process. For if they hold that the process and the Agreement have already transported the two communities in Northern Ireland to a better and far happier place, who do they think was in the co-pilot's seat?

Could he have done more? And maybe better? Did he make mistakes? And, perhaps, sometimes make enemies too easily? There is no doubt that in the heat of a particular moment Trimble would explode spectacularly, so feeding his "angry man" image and those unflattering descriptions of his inter-personal skills. But even senior civil servants who had been at the end of a tongue-lashing would subsequently confirm that Trimble is not a man to bear grudges. As one puts it eloquently: "Trimble is not a hater." Could he be angular and difficult? Of course. Was he sometimes erratic, emotional and unsure? Absolutely. And who placed in his position would not be?

But did he play a major part — at arguably greater personal danger to himself even than that run by Gerry Adams — in bringing the two communities to a place where the British and Irish governments, the Americans and world opinion at large believed they needed to be taken? The verdict on that cannot be in doubt.

On the historical balance sheet there will be a more equivocal verdict about Trimble's success in moving unionism to that other place.

There are enduring questions and criticisms about his party management style — or, as some would say, lack of it. However, it should in fairness be observed that he could hardly have survived the repeated challenges to his leadership without devoting considerably more time to managing his party than may have been apparent to those of us on the outside. His supporters suggest this in turn invites the conclusion that he was in fact therefore probably more successful in managing his party than conventional wisdom allows.

Trimble wanted to break his party's historic links with the Orange Order and to re-create a more pluralist party. But he didn't have the votes to do it. Even his closest allies would complain that he was too indulgent of the dissident Jeffrey Donaldson from the outset. But could he really be blamed for not wanting to preside over a formal split which, when it finally came, would consolidate Ian Paisley's "anti-Agreement" unionist majority? Indeed he would in turn be open to the charge that he finally facilitated the DUP's triumph by seeking to expel Donaldson, along with MPs David Burnside and the Rev Martin Smyth following their resignation of the party whip at Westminster.

It had hardly seemed to be the business of a leader to be expelling half his parliamentary party, not to mention in Donaldson his party's biggest vote-winner. Indeed particularly so because it was a fair bet that Blair would finally bow to the pressure to hold fresh elections in any event, and that — notwithstanding Gerry Adams's more generous assessment of him — republicans would not deliver for Trimble when they had good reason to anticipate that he would lose to Paisley. By that stage of course the Ulster Unionists had fought their internal battles to a point of exhaustion, where they appeared to the wider unionist electorate and the world beyond to be more or less dysfunctional.

Who will take the blame for that? And will it matter? Trimble will have the support of outsiders looking on to whom it was simply inexplicable that Donaldson could reject majority decision after majority decision of his party colleagues and return to the fray, perpetuating the internal party divisions notoriously disliked by voters. Internal unionist critics will argue to the contrary that Trimble's margin of advantage, certainly in the later stages, was an insufficient basis to continue with the project. The force behind this was that the numbers then against him inside the UUP, taken together with the DUP and other fringe parties, indicated that majority unionist consent for the Agreement had in fact been withdrawn over the period after the 1998 referendum. Then again, as his friends argued at the time, where was Trimble to turn? And which would carry greater sway with the governments in London, Dublin and Washington? A majority of unionists, by then against the Agreement — or a majority of all the people of Northern Ireland and the overwhelming majority of the people of the Republic who had voted in favour? Indeed there is interesting discussion here about who and what might in future constitute "the majority" in Northern Ireland, at least for the purpose of determining how it should be governed.

In purely party terms, one Trimble supporter offers the benign suggestion that it might finally be concluded that Trimble and Donaldson were jointly culpable, in that they failed to get beyond the personal and deal with the essential political business. And for reasons already rehearsed here, it may not matter very much in the end. For following Jeffrey Donaldson's final break with the UUP, the talk is of a further realignment within unionism in a "post-Paisley" and "post-Trimble" era, a development which even some fervent supporters of the Agreement think an inevitable response to Sinn Féin's ascendancy within Northern nationalism and its growing prospects in the Irish Republic.

Moreover — and notwithstanding its insistence that it will be negotiating a "new" agreement — by autumn of 2004, the newly ascendant Democratic Unionist Party had already said and published enough to encourage hope in London and Dublin that it would in time accommodate itself to the basic architecture and underlying principles of the Belfast Agreement.

At this writing certainly it would be too much to expect those who think to have vanquished Trimble and his party to acknowledge their debt to him for all the "heavy lifting", or the inherent truth of Gerry Adams's assertion that the DUP has the comparatively easy part to play if it chooses to do so.

However, an important point was made by Niall O'Dowd in an article in *The Irish Times* on 30 August 2004, when he said it was well past the time for Ulster Unionists to stop their own begrudgery about the part played in this peace process by President Clinton and by leading Irish Americans. Much of it is actually rooted in memory of the controversies engendered at an earlier stage in the process, for example over President Clinton's decision to over-rule British government objections and grant that first American visa to Gerry Adams.

Again, in fairness, we should recall the context in which such issues were so hotly disputed as one in which unionists feared a republican trick and suspected the peace process might represent the ultimate refinement of the "armalite and ballot box" strategy.

Just as they were ever fearful of secret deals between the Provisionals and the British, so too — and understandably enough at the time perhaps — so many unionists were suspicious and wary about the involvement of significant figures in the Irish American community in sponsoring the peace process. However, the Ulster Unionists have long since adapted themselves to that process, indeed claimed part ownership of it, and it is absurd for them to then cling to prejudices or impressions formed at an earlier point. They didn't like the fact of the Hume/Adams dialogue. But can they imagine the process would have got under way if somebody, somewhere hadn't started the talking? They didn't like President Clinton's visa decision, and couldn't have been expected to at the time. But do they really feel anger about it still — still think that this somehow retarded the process rather than helped consolidate it? They didn't much care for former Taoiseach Albert Reynolds, or the enthusiasm and disregard for British process with which he urged on Prime Minister John Major. But can anybody who has since bought the deal now deny that his government too was running risks for peace? Or, for all that he infuriated them, that former Tánaiste Dick Spring played a significant role — if at times to unionists a seemingly conflicting one — first alongside Taoiseach Reynolds and then alongside Taoiseach John Bruton?

Not every decision made would have been the right one. And unionists were naturally and rightly on the alert for any evidence that government systems in London or Dublin were being in any sense corrupted by the enthusiasm of ministers and officials to cut a deal with former terrorists. They will also feel justified in their view that London, Dublin and Washington have continued to be needlessly indulgent of Irish republicans in the changed world post-11 September 2001. But viewed in the round, and with the benefit of hindsight, weren't these decisions by Clinton and others simply precursors to the sort of fudges, compromises and tough calls which the Ulster Unionists themselves would later be required to make and for which they would plead understanding?

Peace-making requires courage. It also at some stage requires something of the generosity of the human spirit. And it is helped take root through the process of learning and mutual discovery which comes when enemies decide to make peace, and from the ongoing process of re-evaluation and re-assessment which that invites. Just as the unionists would do well to heed this point, so, too, many think David Trimble might also expect to feel rather more of that generous spirit.

At minimum, I hope his account here provides a fuller understanding of the struggles, pressures and constraints he faced as he sought to advance the ambitions of his own people, while simultaneously seeking to assuage their fears and anxieties and at the same time proffer political reward to those who promised to lead Irish republicans away from armed struggle.

However, I actually think it does more than that. Trimble stoutly maintains that he never abandoned his policy of "no guns, no government" but rather fought for it, time and again, right up to the fourth suspension of the Assembly in October 2003. And that is true. Yet it strikes me as not quite the whole truth. By acknowledging the "opacities" in the Belfast Agreement, I think he confirms that he did much more in fact to advance the process, and to allow it to breathe and grow, than he would or could have claimed at the time.

The legitimate unionist concern would be expressed from time to time that Trimble had lost his necessary independence as an Ulster Unionist leader, and bought too much into "British state thinking". Yet as his victorious unionist enemies moved progressively onto the same ground, Trimble loyalists would retort that his only crime was "joined-up thinking".

One of his great strengths certainly was that he did not confuse perceptions with facts, and was prepared constantly to revise his position in the light of the available evidence. However, I think the conclusion inescapable that Trimble did at times prioritise the peace process and the preservation of the Agreement above the narrower interests of his party. He may well baulk at this, but it is hard to come to any other conclusion on the evidence of the risks he ran. Certainly it is difficult to imagine a politician concerned above all with party battling on for the Agreement as his internal majority withered while the external enemy stormed the gates. In such conditions, "No Surrender" might easily have represented the easier option. David Trimble, however, was sustained by the conviction this was a deal of which his great political hero Sir James Craig would have approved.

Depending on future outcomes, career-orientated Ulster Unionists in particular might never forgive him for it. However, when the historical judgement comes to be written I think the conclusion will be that Trimble was a remarkably non-political politician who showed a distinct reluctance at times to press for party advantage. This is not to suggest that he casually or unthinkingly threw away his party's majority, or that he in any sense thought to sacrifice his party for the greater good of the Agreement. To the contrary, Trimble was consumed by the party and convinced, given his disdain for the DUP, that the UUP was the only possible vehicle to sustain the Agreement. By the time self-confessed "hubris" set in in the summer and autumn of 2003, he was also clearly — if unwisely — driven by the belief that only the successful restoration of the devolved administration would give him a fighting chance of electoral victory. And the result on the actual day, giving 30 seats to the Democratic Unionists and 27 to Ulster Unionists, was itself pretty remarkable given the circumstances and immediate backdrop of that failed negotiation with Adams. This certainly did not represent (at least yet) a "meltdown" of the kind experienced by the SDLP, and Trimble is defiant here of those who insist a DUP/Sinn Féin "two-party state" is either inevitable or an already accomplished fact.

At this writing, the dynamics still seem to favour further unionist realignment. But whatever about the future course of events within unionism, the fact remains that for Trimble — as for "the mandarins" in the Northern Ireland Office — the highest priority was to achieve manageable and sustainable outcomes of benefit to the whole of society in Northern Ireland. Indeed, it seems unmistakable that, had it been otherwise, this process could not have journeyed so fast, so soon. And in that sense Trimble was arguably a lot less "tribal" in his approach to politics than Tony Blair.

So, yes — and for some reasons that he will not necessarily recognise or accept — they really did make history on that Good Friday 1998, and they really could not have done it without David Trimble.

Index